Chenrezig

Embodying Compassionate Presence

Also by Rob Preece

The Wisdom of Imperfection: The Challenge of Individuation in Buddhist Life

The Psychology of Buddhist Tantra

The Courage to Feel: Buddhist Practices for Opening to Others

Preparing for Tantra: Creating the Psychological Ground for Practice

Feeling Wisdom: Working with Emotions Using Buddhist Teachings and Western Psychology

Tasting the Essence of Tantra: Buddhist Meditation for Contemporary Western Life

The Mandala and Visions of Wholeness: Within Tibetan Buddhism and Jungian Psychology

Heart Essence: Enhancing Qualities of the Awakening Mind

Chenrezig

Embodying Compassionate Presence

Rob Preece

Mudra Publications
Devon, 2023

Mudra Publications
1 Church Park Cottages
Holne
Devon TQ13 7SG
UK.

www.mudra.co.uk

ISBN: 978-1-7399402-2-5

Edited by Diane Schaap

Cover design by Rob Preece

Contents

Preface

The Essence of Tantra Series

Tantric practice is a profound approach to the complete transformation and liberation of our body, speech and mind from what limits and obscures their natural potential. Often, the visualisation of colourful and inspiring deities is considered central to this way of practice. This is partly true – but tantric practice is so much more when we fully understand how it 'works'. Tantra becomes a way of integrating many different aspects of our life into a radical process of awakening. Our mind, our emotional and psychological life, our creative life, our body and relationships are all aspects of this process. All that we are is included within this path of alchemical transformation.

In this *Essence of Tantra Series* of books, following on from *Tasting the Essence of Tantra*, I will be looking at particular aspects of tantric practice in more detail. Much of the material included in these books has grown out of the four-year *Tasting the Essence of Tantra* series of modules I taught in Europe, the US and the UK over the past twelve years. These modules gave me the opportunity to gather together the essential ingredients of tantric practice and explore how effective they are in relation to our contemporary life and psychological nature. It also provided the opportunity to explore a way of practice that was much more deeply rooted in the body and the process of meditation rather than being oriented towards the recitation of *sadhana* texts.

The word *tantra* in Sanskrit is often translated as 'weave'. When we go more deeply into the nature of tantric practice, we discover a weave or matrix of ways of transformation and healing that are profound and, in many ways, radical. In this series of books, I will explore an approach to personal transformation that has particular significance for our contemporary psychological life. The practices I will introduce represent a healing matrix that can address some of the key psychological challenges many of us can experience in our lives. These are practices that can also enable us to awaken qualities that are at the heart of a bodhisattva's capacity to manifest in the world whatever is beneficial for the welfare of others.

Some books in this series will focus on specific deity practices; others will explore significant aspects of tantra such as the nature of the mandala and the cultivation of bodhicitta, the awakening heart essence, as it relates to tantric practice. During this process I will also introduce certain meditations which are intended to demonstrate the creative nature of tantric practice. This is a reflection of how I was taught by my primary teacher Lama Thubten Yeshe, who saw that tantra could be explored in a creative way. Much of what I draw upon here comes from the richness of experience this more creative approach can bring and how it can specifically address our psychological disposition as Westerners. I have been involved in these practices for almost 50 years and have spent a great deal of time in retreat teaching and guiding others. Through that experience I have discovered many ways in which tantric practice can transform and awaken our inner reality. It can be an extraordinary gift and presence in our life. In each of these books I will remain true to the essence of the tantric path, and I wish to bring to that path a freshness in how we can integrate it in our lives. What primarily interests me is how we each can experience tantra as a living inner process, not just the technicalities of a system of practices. This series of books gives me the opportunity to explore this extraordinary path through two lenses: the profound richness of the Tibetan tradition as well as invaluable insights that come from my Jungian psychology background. My hope is that the confluence of these perspectives will enrich and inspire your journey as it has my own.

Dedication

I dedicate this book to all those who have supported me with their compassion, kindness and understanding through my life's journey.

I also would like to dedicate this to those I have worked with in the context of psychotherapy and mentoring, whose experiences and challenges have been a huge source of insight and inspiration.

May your lives be free of suffering and endowed with happiness and its causes.

Chenrezig: The Buddha of Compassion

Introduction

FOR ANYONE who begins to explore the Buddhist world, perhaps the most familiar deity they will meet is the buddha of compassion – known in Tibet as Chenrezig, in India as Avalokiteshvara and in China as Guanyin. For the Tibetans in particular, Chenrezig is hugely significant primarily because H.H. Dalai Lama is considered the embodiment of Chenrezig in the human world. It is very common to hear Tibetan lay people, walking along with malas (rosaries) in their hands, quietly muttering the mantra of Chenrezig: OM MANI PADME HUNG. Their devotion to both the Dalai Lama and Chenrezig is a profoundly supportive presence in their lives.

Many lay Tibetans who have not had the opportunity to have formal education within the monasteries often hold the view that Chenrezig is a god that has manifested in the world to serve sentient beings out of his great compassion. The Dalai Lama then holds the place of a god incarnated. Those who have been through a deeper education into the principles of Buddhist philosophy will not see Chenrezig as a god, but rather as an aspect of our innate buddha-nature that we can each awaken. The Dalai Lama then becomes a man who has gradually awoken to that innate buddha potential and is able to embody the qualities of Chenrezig in the world to serve others.

The primary quality that Chenrezig embodies is *mahakaruna*, "great compassion". As I have said, Chenrezig is seen as the buddha of compassion, but he is also sometimes described as the bodhisattva of compassion and this has a subtly different connotation. We understand a bodhisattva as one who aspires to fully awaken in order to liberate sentient beings from suffering. A bodhisattva's heart intention, known as bodhicitta or the awakening mind, is rooted in two ingredients. The first of these is a deeply felt compassion for the suffering of all sentient beings; the second is the knowledge of our potential to awaken to our innate buddha-nature. This combination is a powerful cocktail that gives a bodhisattva the courage and determination to take on the challenges of the path to awaken to serve others. Chenrezig could be said to personify or symbolise the deep sense of compassionate bodhicitta that a bodhisattva holds in the heart towards all living creatures. Hence he is known as the bodhisattva of compassion.

There is a very dynamic aspect of compassion that energetically seeks to eliminate the suffering of another and will actively engage in the world to do so. But there is also another side to compassion, one I wish to call *compassionate presence*, that is often more subtle and nuanced. As I have found in my work as a psychotherapist, compassionate presence is possibly the most healing quality we can offer another. The quality of our parents' holding as we enter into this life is very significant in how safe and comfortable we feel as we grow. Our parents' capacity to offer compassionate presence and love to us as an infant, and from the moment of conception through birth and into our early years of life, can determine how we develop our sense of self. For many of us this early experience was not ideal and we may have lacked the safe compassionate environment we needed. As children, our sensitivity to the undercurrents and emotional dynamics of the environment in which we grow up can have a considerable impact upon us. As a consequence, we will often introject an inner environment that is not kind and compassionate. but harsh, anxious and critical. When we lack self-compassion, it can also be a challenge to hold a sense of compassion towards those we live amongst and work amongst.

In so many aspects of our life, the need for compassion and kindness is important but often lacking. In our working environment, when compassion is present we can more easily relax and be ourselves with our qualities and our difficulties. A compassionate environment brings a feeling of safety and trust; we can be more open and responsive to others we work with and allow vulnerability to be acceptable. We can feel supported and comfortable knowing we don't have to be perfect or always do the right thing to be acceptable. When compassion is absent in our work environment, it will often feel unsafe, threatening, competitive and aggressive. People will be more reactive, insecure and stressed, feeling the need to perform or defend themselves to justify their value and acceptability. Vulnerability and the need for support is then unacceptable, and the need to appear competent is crucial.

A world pervaded by the presence of compassion could be an extraordinary place and, as H.H. Dalai Lama wrote in his book *Beyond Religion,*[1] we could all be much happier, healthier, and less stressed and insecure. Within the Buddhist tradition, compassion is considered perhaps the most important quality we can cultivate. This is often emphasised in our relationship to others but is equally important in our relationship to ourselves – where it can often be lacking. Within the tantric tradition, Chenrezig is one of the primary deities that support the awakening of our innate potential for compassionate presence towards both self and others.

We first meet the presence of Chenrezig in India when, as Avalokiteshvara, he was one of the leading disciples of the Buddha, renowned for his role in voicing the *Heart Sutra*. Over time, however, a shift began to happen; Avalokiteshvara "evolved" from being a venerated disciple of the Buddha to a revered deity that embodies the bodhisattva's ideal of compassion. In the deity Chenrezig we recognise a sublime manifestation of compassionate presence that can become an important resource in our lives.

Today the main source of the Chenrezig practice comes from Tibet. In the Tibetan tradition there are many different forms of Chenrezig as well as ways of practice. Within this book I will focus upon the familiar four-armed aspect as the primary source. Over the many years of being involved in this practice both personally and in teaching others, I have increasingly discovered ways of meditation that can suit our Western disposition. In the West we are psychologically very different to the Tibetans and have very different needs in terms of healing and transformation. I am aware that as young Tibetans move out into the world this difference may be less marked. However, in my own experience and through the experience of those I teach, I have increasingly seen how this practice can be brought alive to meet our own psychological process.

The practice of Chenrezig is a weave or matrix of creative ways of meditation that can respond to and potentially heal and transform many aspects of our psychological wounding. In this book I wish to particularly look at the root of much of the suffering we experience in our lives – suffering that is often the result of early emotional wounding. I will emphasise the way in which compassionate presence is important in the gradual healing and transformation of that root of suffering, to bring a deeper sense of well-being from which to live our lives. It is through this inner healing that we can then begin to truly open to our natural potential to feel compassion for others and hold them also with compassionate presence. The deepening experience of Chenrezig helps facilitate this healing and also enables our capacity for compassion to grow to its natural fruition of bodhicitta and the bodhisattva's way of life.

In this book I will describe many ways of meditation that grow out of a very simple basic form. My intention is to offer ways that may enable some of our core wounding to begin to heal so that we can be ready and able to embody the qualities of a bodhisattva in the world to serve others. If you find these practices helpful in addressing some of your own inner process, let them become a resource in your life. Many of the insights in my understanding of the practice of Chenrezig have come from the responses and experience of those I have taught and mentored. For this I am truly grateful. I have also always felt guided by the inspiration of H.H. Dalai Lama who was one of my main teachers when I lived in Dharamsala. He is such a clean, clear embodiment of compassion manifesting in the world. He is a genuine inspiration of how our practice of Chenrezig can draw us closer to gradually embodying compassionate presence in our lives in whatever way is most beneficial.

1

Who is Chenrezig?

THE DEITY known in Sanskrit as Avalokiteshvara, "the lord who gazes down at the cries of the world" – or in Tibetan as Chenrezig, "he who looks upon all beings with the eyes of compassion" – is said to embody the universal compassion of a bodhisattva. It is sometimes said that Chenrezig is the buddha of compassion, but it is perhaps helpful to see him as embodying the archetypal intent of a bodhisattva's compassion. It is through the practice of Chenrezig that we will begin to deepen our own experience of the innate compassion within us and its transformation into the intention of bodhicitta, the awakening mind or heart essence.

Throughout Buddhist history and literature there are numerous references to Avalokiteshvara. He is often seen as one of the most important disciples of the Buddha and his role as a highly evolved bodhisattva is exemplary. He is the one through whom the perfection of wisdom sutra, known as the *Heart Sutra,* is conveyed. The Buddha is said to have instigated the dialogue between Avalokiteshvara and another disciple, Shariputra, who asks the question:

"How should the perfection of wisdom be practiced as a bodhisattva?" Avalokiteshvara replies on the Buddha's behalf in the form of what is now well known as the Heart Sutra.

Avalokiteshvara appears in the illustrations of the wheel of life where, in the form of a monk, he brings the necessary quality of the Dharma to the six realms of existence to free beings there from the cycle of samsara. Here he exemplifies the extraordinary quality of a bodhisattva's compassionate presence, ready to enter into the different realms of suffering to liberate beings. As I will describe in chapter 3, in each realm he is depicted carrying an object which represents what those in that realm need in order to be free of suffering.

As Buddhism entered Tibet, various manifestations emerged of what has now become Chenrezig, less associated with the original historical figure of Avalokiteshvara and more as a tantric deity. I will focus on the nature of Chenrezig as a deity in this book rather than on Chenrezig as an historical presence in the Buddha's entourage. Amongst Tibetans and Western Tibetan Buddhists, the Dalai Lama is considered to be the embodiment of Chenrezig. Other lamas are also considered in this way, which may lead to some confusion if we do not understand what that means. We might wonder who is the *true* embodiment, or who is *more* an embodiment? If we consider, however, that each of us has within us the innate potential of Chenrezig as an archetypal expression of pure compassion, then we could all come to embody Chenrezig. If we do this deity practice with sufficient dedication and meditative focus, we can awaken this potential and actually become the embodiment of compassion. The Dalai Lama is one person for whom it is said this quality is fully manifest and that he is therefore a perfect conduit for the archetypal nature of Chenrezig to be embodied in the world. Of course, other lamas can do the same – just as, with practice, each of us could.

Over time there have been many manifestations of Chenrezig within the Tibetan Buddhist world. The most familiar is the form known as four-arm Chenrezig. There is also the thousand-arm aspect, as well as other six-arm forms. While the most familiar form is seated, many forms are standing. In an extraordinary transformation of Avalokiteshvara as this expression of compassion moved to China and Japan, a female aspect emerged: in China, Guanyin, and in Japan, Kannon. Within the tantric world of Tibet there are also wrathful manifestations of Chenrezig as Dharma protectors in various forms of Mahakala.

When we look at the images of Chenrezig we may naturally feel a resonance with the quality or attributes he embodies or symbolises. With Chenrezig we come into relationship with a particular flavour of compassion that can be awakened through bringing to life and actualising this quality in our being. As I have said, possibly the most familiar form, the one we are going to explore here, is the four-arm aspect (see front cover). Chenrezig's white colour, his sitting posture and the mudras, or gestures, of his hands all have significance. The particular objects that he is holding in his hands also have profound symbolic meaning. Perhaps the first thing to notice is that there is a natural balance in the form of Chenrezig that is not evident in many other iconographical images. In the process of painting a thangka of any deity, the very first line that is usually drawn is known as the Brahma line, which runs down the centre of the painting like a central axis. This line is like the central fulcrum of our being, from which we move into form and engage in life. Chenrezig noticeably sits in complete balance along this axis, in a symmetry that is actually quite uncommon in tantric deities. I have written about this balance in *Heart Essence* in relationship to the brahmavihara of equanimity [2]. Psychologically this conveys a sense of being utterly aligned and still, in this balanced place of being. Nothing goes out of alignment, and if something causes this quality to be momentarily knocked off centre it naturally returns to that place of wholeness and balance that deep compassion and equanimity can bring. I am reminded of the little toys that have a round bottom so that, when you knock them, they rock and roll around and come naturally back to a place of stable equilibrium. Compassionate presence, when centred in this way, holds a place of equilibrium and balance that is not disturbed by bias and partiality. I will explore this further in chapter 6.

Still and present yet touched by the suffering in the world, Chenrezig exudes a warmth that is expressed partly by his colour. He is white and radiant, reflecting a clean, clear nature that is free of stains and defilements, yet his body has a subtle pink glow. This is not the cold, icy blue-white found in the arctic. It is a white that conveys warmth and relationship rather than cold detachment. This pink glow has a connection to a quality that is not bound by suffering but is also blissful as a result of the inner awakening of the mind's nature.

In the four-arm aspect of Chenrezig we see his first two hands held at the heart with palms together holding a small piece of lapis lazuli. This mudra is rich in symbolic meaning. If we place our hands together at the heart and feel into the quality of that gesture, we can begin to sense its meaning. It is a familiar gesture to anyone who has been to Nepal. The Nepalese are always putting palms together in this way and saying *namaste,* which could be translated as *homage to the divine within you.* This gesture is sometimes called the prostration mudra and it has various attributed meanings. It can be seen as the union of two facets of our nature: wisdom and compassion, both necessary to the awakening path. It is sometimes considered that the fingers and thumbs together symbolise the ten grounds or stages of the bodhisattva's path. The eight fingers themselves represent the eightfold path.

Despite these meanings, we can actually feel the quality of the gesture. There is something very warm and heart-felt about placing the palms together at the heart before another person. It can be a gesture of honour and respect and at the same time humbling as we gently bow towards another. This mudra of Chenrezig with the hands held together at the heart has an added symbolic ingredient, a small piece of lapis lazuli held between the palms.

The symbolism of this piece of blue lapis lazuli is very interesting. You may be familiar with lapis lazuli as a semi-precious stone which played a significant part in medieval alchemy throughout Europe and the Middle East. Lapis was sometimes seen as the *philosopher's stone* or one of the symbols of the result of alchemical transformation. In this process it represented the final emergence of the innate purity of the alchemist's nature as a process of awakening.

In the symbolism of Chenrezig, lapis lazuli is particularly associated with bodhicitta, the innate purity of the heart essence awakened through the cultivation of compassion and love. When this quality emerges, it is a natural and potent intention that carries us towards full awakening like a river flowing towards the sea. Bodhicitta transforms our being into the awakened nature of a buddha, bringing with it extraordinary gifts dedicated to the welfare of others. Shantideva in *Bodhisattvacaryavatara,* or *Guide to the Bodhisattva's Way of Life*, describes bodhicitta as "the supreme gold-making elixir, for it transforms the unclean body we have taken into the priceless jewel of a buddha form."[3] The natural outflow from the heart of bodhicitta becomes a powerful catalyst of transformation in the alchemical process culminating in the lapis lazuli as the philosopher's stone.

Taking the exploration of Chenrezig's form further, we see that he has a second right hand holding a crystal rosary and a second left hand holding a pink lotus flower. The crystal rosary in his right hand represents the power of his pure speech. In this case we also understand that pure speech particularly refers to the mantra of great compassion, OM MANI PADME HUNG. This mantra will be familiar to anyone who has been around the Tibetan Buddhist world; it is a constant background of Tibetan peoples' lives, especially within the lay community. The mantra of great compassion has a very simple meaning, the "jewel within the lotus", but as I will explain in chapter 3 the underlying nature of this mantra has much deeper implications.

Chenrezig's second left hand holds a pink lotus flower blooming at the left side of his head. The symbolism of this lotus relates to the nature of Chenrezig's mind. His mind is pure, clear and free of defilement like a lotus that arises from the mud of samsara yet is pure and clean. The implication is that the innate nature of the heart-mind is pure though temporarily obscured by the mud of our confusion and suffering. But this obscuration never defiles the actual nature of our mind which can arise free of defilement, clean, clear and radiant. This mind is a blend of pristine awareness and the spontaneous presence of compassion.

One final symbol in Chenrezig's appearance, one that can sometimes seem a little incongruous, is the antelope skin he wears across his shoulder. A story is told of a bodhisattva manifesting in the aspect of an antelope that was willing to sacrifice itself for the welfare of a sentient being. This action of extraordinary kindness and compassion is honoured by Chenrezig wearing the skin of the antelope. The antelope is also considered a symbol of gentleness.

When we meditate upon the deity Chenrezig, we are bringing into our awareness his sambhogakaya aspect with all of its symbolic attributes. His appearance is a direct emanation of the pure energy-body of the buddhas that is also intimately connected to our own innate buddha-nature. If we consider all these symbolic attributes expressed in the form of Chenrezig, we begin to recognise how he exemplifies the awakening nature of a bodhisattva dedicated to serve the welfare of others. In the meditations I will introduce, we begin to explore many different ways in which we can cultivate our relationship to this sambhogakaya quality and bring it into our experience as the embodiment of compassionate presence.

2

The Bodhisattva Chenrezig

CHENREZIG IS AMONG a number of tantric deities who are seen as fully awakened buddhas but can equally be recognised as bodhisattvas. Three deities are seen as primary reflections of a bodhisattva's quality manifesting in the world for the welfare of others. Manjushri can be considered the embodiment of a bodhisattva's capacity for the communication and expression of wisdom. Vajrapani is considered the power of the awakening mind of a bodhisattva to be effective in liberating others from suffering. Chenrezig could be seen as a bodhisattva's fundamental capacity of compassionate presence. The combination of these three reflects the integration of what is needed for a bodhisattva to be sensitive to the suffering of others, to have insight into what is needed to alleviate that suffering and to then be effective in doing so.

Compassion is the very core of a bodhisattva's *raison d'être*. Were it not for our natural human capacity to respond to the suffering of others with a sense of empathy and compassion, there would not be a basis from which bodhicitta grows. It is often said in traditional teachings such as Shantideva's *"Guide"* that without compassion there would be no buddhas. It is the primary cause from which the desire to awaken and relieve others from suffering arises. This capacity may be so fundamental to our human potential that, without it, the world would be a bleak and hostile place to live. To be aware of this we only have to recall the atrocities of Nazi Germany during the second world war or the Russian invasion of Ukraine at the time of writing this book. While we all have the potential for compassion, a bodhisattva cultivates this quality in a way that makes it an extraordinary force for good. It becomes a primary spark that ignites the fire of bodhicitta in our hearts.

With extraordinary compassion, Chenrezig gazes upon the world of suffering. Out of a tear from his eye is born the active ingredient of compassion in the form of the goddess Green Tara, who steps into the world to liberate sentient beings. Chenrezig himself is not necessarily the active ingredient of compassion but rather the capacity to be utterly present with the suffering of the world and allow it to touch deeply into our being. This is *compassionate presence*, a profoundly significant quality of a bodhisattva.

Because of this great compassion that feels the suffering of the world to be so painful, a bodhisattva chooses to remain in embodied life rather than seeking release from the cycle of birth and death. In Buddhism there are two primary paths. One path leads to the state of extinction known as the arhant. This is one who, through a renunciation of "worldly life", cultivates an extraordinary capacity of meditation that extinguishes any karmic propensities to be born into an embodied form within the cycle of existence. This state of total liberation is something a bodhisattva finds unthinkable so long as there are sentient beings suffering in the world. The second path is to then remain embodied and incarnated for the welfare of others. The monk Togme Zangpo, in a text called *The 37 practices of all Buddhas' sons (and daughters)*, reflects:

> *In each incarnation, through all of our lives,*
> *We have been cared for by others with motherly love.*
> *While these mothers of ours are still lost in samsara,*
> *How cruel to ignore them and free but ourself!*
> *To save other beings though countless in number,*
> *To free from their sorry these mothers of old,*
> *Produce bodhicitta, the wish to be Buddha –*
> *The children of the Buddhas all practice this way.*[4]

This sentiment is often reflected in the question: how could someone swim to the shore of a lake when they know their mother is still in the water drowning? Such a basic denial of the suffering of others would be intolerable.

A bodhisattva chooses to remain in the world and bear the hardship of working to liberate others from suffering. For this to be possible it is necessary to abide, in effect, between two realities. To be with the reality of the relative environment of engagement in the normal challenges of life while opening to an awareness of the ultimate nature of our reality. This life between form and emptiness, between embodiment and clear open awareness, is in a continual creative play of expression. This interplay enables a bodhisattva to find the inner resources of clarity and wisdom combined with the courage to manifest the quality of compassion in the world. Chenrezig could be said to sit on that threshold between form and emptiness where he is an expression of the energetic dynamic of manifestation. Chenrezig embodies the fundamental capacity for compassionate presence that feels and witnesses the suffering of the world.

If we consider a bodhisattva from a tantric point of view, this threshold between form and emptiness can be described in a subtly different way. At the heart of our understating of tantra is the relationship between what are called the three *kayas*[5], or bodies, as three aspects of our innate buddha-nature. The first of these three is *dharmakaya*, the primordial purity of the mind's empty nature. This is sometimes seen as the *ground of being* from which all appearances manifest, yet it is beyond forms and concepts. The second is *sambhogakaya*, the primordially pure nature of the energy-body known as *the enjoyment body* but sometimes called the emotional body because in our ordinary nature it is felt in the dimension of our emotional life. The third is *nirmanakaya*, the emanation or manifestation body. This is our physical body which becomes the vehicle through which the other two manifest and emanate (see Figure 1).

In our ordinary life these three kayas are still present, but in their relatively un-evolved condition; mind is busy thinking and often overactive, our energy-body is permeated by emotional reaction and our physical body has abilities as well as health difficulties. A tantric bodhisattva is gradually cultivating and refining these three kayas, liberating them from their ordinary condition. It is the interplay between these three that can then begin to be experienced as the movement from the subtle level of mind into the dynamic energy of intention and expression, finally coming into form and embodiment. A bodhisattva gradually comes to embody this dynamic as a conduit or channel for buddha-nature to manifest in the world to liberate others from suffering.

Chenrezig sits in the heart of this process as a catalyst that transforms the energy-body, or sambhogakaya, into a powerful presence of compassion. The gradual awakening of Chenrezig in our energetic nature enables us to begin to emanate his quality of heart-essence bodhicitta. This means his archetypal bodhisattva quality will enhance and empower our own capacity to manifest a natural compassionate presence in our work, our relationships and how we respond to the world around.

Our relationship to Chenrezig can be an extraordinary resource as we embark upon the life of a bodhisattva working in the world. This resource can come in two ways. One is that we can bring into our lives the compassion of all the buddhas as a holding presence to support us when we need help and guidance. This could be seen as the emanation of the buddhas as a *wisdom being* in whom we take refuge and to whom we make our prayers and offer our gratitude for the support we receive. The second is in the way we gradually discover our own *inner* resource as our innate Chenrezig nature becomes increasingly awake and present. He is an emanation of our buddha-nature that enables us to manifest what can be truly beneficial in our lives for the welfare of others and of the life of the planet. He supports us to gradually yet fully become the bodhisattva that we can be in this life, with the courage and compassion to remain in the world. As Shantideva said: *"For as long as space endures, and for as long as sentient beings remain, until then may I too remain to dispel the miseries of the world."*[6]

Figure 1

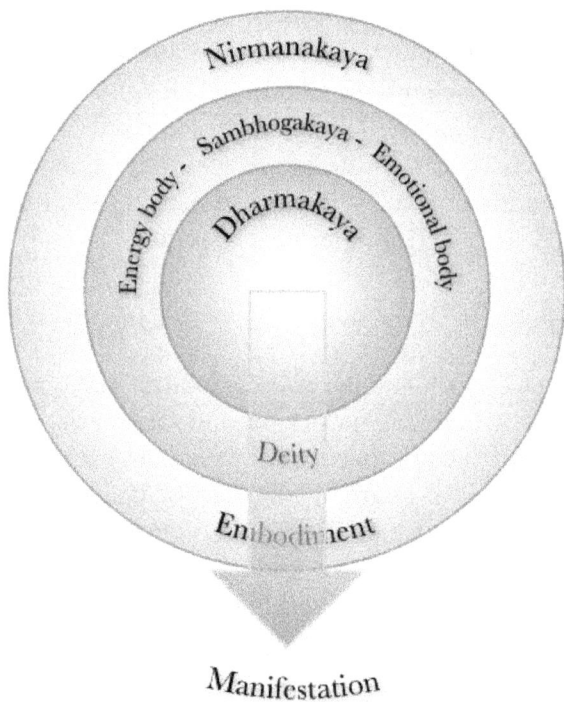

(This diagram is derived from one within the MA dissertation of Anna Murray Preece 2017)

3

The Mantra of Great Compassion

I HAVE DESCRIBED CHENREZIG as a primary expression of a bodhisattva's willingness to remain embodied in the world to serve the welfare of others. From an Eastern perspective, found in both Buddhism and the Hindu tradition, the world is not made up of just the familiar human and animal kingdoms. Within the cycle of existence, or *samsara* as it is called in Sanskrit, the suffering of sentient beings is described on six levels. These are known as the *deva* or god realm, the *asura* or demi-god realm, the human and animal realms, the *preta* or wandering spirit realm and finally the *narak* or hell realm. For a Buddhist, Chenrezig, as the manifestation of the bodhisattva's compassion, is said to be willing to step into each of the realms of cyclic existence to liberate beings from suffering. From a Buddhist point of view, each of the six realms has a particular karmic cause, like a seed potential that abides in our continuum and can ripen into that reality. The power of Chenrezig's compassion to alleviate suffering in these realms is expressed in the mantra OM MANI PADME HUNG, possibly the most familiar and famous mantra within the entire Tibetan tradition. The energetic nature of the six syllables OM MA NI PAD ME HUNG is said to have the power to purify and neutralise these six seed potentials.

Each of these syllables combines a sound and a particular colour. OM is white and purifies the seed of the *deva* realm and its delusional nature of pride. MA is green and purifies the seed of the *asura* or demi-god realm and its delusion of jealousy and competitiveness. NI is a golden colour associated with the human realm and purifies the delusion of desire. Sky-blue PAD (pronounced *pad* in Sanskrit and *pay* by the Tibetans) purifies the ignorance associated with the animal realm. ME is red in colour and purifies the seed of craving associated with the *preta* or hungry ghost realm. Finally, deep-blue HUNG purifies the delusion of hatred and fear associated with the realm of the hell beings.

In paintings of the wheel of life, often found at the entrance of Tibetan temples, we see these six realms depicted in graphic detail. In Buddhism these six states of birth within the cycle of existence are usually considered to be literal locations where we can be reborn after we die. The Tibetans hold this view very strongly and often emphasise the idea that recognising the depth of suffering in each of these realms motivates us to strive towards freedom from the cycle of birth and death. It generates a powerful sense of renunciation often based upon a strong fear that there is no state of birth that gives genuine peaceful happiness, even in the realm of the gods. Within the images of these six realms, a figure that represents Chenrezig is also present, usually standing in the aspect of a monk holding in his hands a particular symbolic object that reflects a quality that liberates those beings from suffering.

While traditionally these six realms are taken very literally, many choose to see them as psychological states that each of us could inhabit even within this human life. As I describe these realms I will try to make that distinction explicit, looking at how these realms can manifest in our human condition.

The Deva Realm

Traditionally the god realm is one where the beings have bodies of radiant light that are resplendent, beautiful and flawless. These beings do not age, they live in an environment that is also pure and beautiful, and they are able to fulfil any desire almost instantly. The gods are characterised by their blissful, inflated self-satisfaction and blindness to suffering. While their lives may be long, it is said that when the karma that sustains them comes to an end their radiance begins to deteriorate and they become aware of their impermanence. They begin to be aware of suffering.

We may recognise the realm of the gods in those within the human world whose lives seem to be so abundantly comfortable that whatever they wish for becomes immediately, effortlessly possible. This is the world of the rich, powerful, wealthy elite and the celebrity, those whose lives can seem to be blessed with good fortune. It is the world of extravagant richness, luxury and stylish sensuality, where people live in grand splendour and opulence that can become self-indulgent, decadent and hedonistic. There can be a kind of inflation and complacent conceit in this world that can feel untouchable or even invincible. There may also be a blindness towards or denial of the suffering of those around who are less fortunate. The tragic hidden shadow is that this world is also transitory, and as we often see in celebrities, glory can easily lead to scandal, ignominy and shame, particularly when the press and media turn upon them.

In this realm we discover an aspect of Chenrezig holding a musical instrument, a vina or lute. Chenrezig as a humble monk becomes a musician whose music is so beautiful and transfixing that it has the power to awaken these self-absorbed gods to the transitory and illusory nature of their reality. Through this music, Chenrezig shows that something beautiful and intoxicating is both transitory and empty and cannot be grasped. The sound of Chenrezig's vina awakens the gods from their complacent absorption and opens their awareness to the emptiness of their world. They see the illusion of all that was held to be so luxurious, elegant and splendid. Waking up from the state of opulent absorption may be the beginning of a change that can make the deva's life less comfortable. This may, on occasion, lead those who begin to recognise their relative good fortune to use it for the benefit of others.

The Asura Realm

In the realm of the asuras, the jealous gods or titans, we enter the world of those who strive to achieve greatness through relentless competition and drive. It is said the asuras are often very warrior-like and caught in a struggle to become dominant and powerful, eventually intending to overthrow the gods whom they see as superior. The asuras are sometimes called the "jealous gods" because their predominant struggle is that they see others who have more glory, more power or more wealth, and wish to have it.

In the human world, this could be the corporate life, where ambition for power and status can be both relentless and ruthless. It could be in the world of politics, where the ambition for power and status is also a major drive. Those who inhabit this realm have big egos that are often aggressively pushing towards their goal at the expense of others, ruthlessly casting people aside to get what they want. They are often very capable and successful high achievers, but at what cost? In this world there is little true wisdom or compassion, only the continual striving of the asura to achieve and the awareness that others may also be ready to stab them in the back. One of the motivating factors for the asura is jealousy of those who have much more prestige and wealth and status, namely the devas. Driven by ambition, the asura will give great attention to the cultivation of those outer signs that will demonstrate their success. The world of the "high-end" consumer is one of the reflections of this success, whether it is the car they drive, the house they live in, the clothing they wear or the executive flights they take. The asura wants to be seen as having the radiance of the gods, and this desire for excellence can be intoxicating and addictive.

In this realm we see an aspect of Chenrezig holding a powerful blazing wisdom sword. The primary concern of those in this world is the ego's ambition for power and dominance. One of the greatest threats to this ego state is the potential for something or someone to be greater, stronger or more powerful. Chenrezig's sword demonstrates a quality of wisdom and power that transcends the jealous god's capacity. It also wakes them up to the limitations of their arrogance and ambition. This can turn the mind and bring greater awareness and the potential to channel all of that striving for power, status and excellence into something more meaningful. This is the *all-accomplishing wisdom* that emerges when the ambitious jealousy is transformed into the capacity to accomplish what is truly beneficial. The striving for excellence that can be an aspect of this asura realm can then become something that may be applied in a beneficial way in the service of others, not just for themselves.

The Animal Realm

If we move into the realm of the animals, we meet creatures that are fundamentally moved by instinct. In the animal kingdom the creatures are totally at home in their body and the environment. They know instinctively how to satisfy their needs for food, for safety and protection against predators, and for procreation. So long as this environment remains stable, they are able to sustain the health and survival of the species very naturally. From a Buddhist perspective we could say that animals live out their karmic propensity naturally and without reflection upon its relative wholesome or unwholesome nature. Animals are seldom likely, it would seem, to act out of the kind of malice and ill will we humans can display. This may mean they kill but they do so without malice. It is just instinct. The closest they may come to displays of aggression out of malice is when protecting their territory or their young, when the instinct to attack is completely natural.

Even within our human life we can recognise this nature. This is how we are when we are very small; when hungry, we instinctively cry in distress until that need is satisfied. Our animal nature is deeply connected to the body and its environment, and how we respond doesn't require thought, it is natural and uncontrived. As adults we can also recognise this instinctual way of being. It is without self-awareness and is pre-reflective. It is the side of us that wants to instinctively gratify its needs to experience pleasure and to be free of pain or discomfort. Unfortunately, in our culture, our animal instinct is often wounded and as a result we can act out behaviour that is destructive and harmful to both self and others. The question will always be: can we wake up and live with it more consciously and healthily?

In the realm of the animals, Chenrezig appears as a monk carrying a text. He is showing the capacity for reflection, for language and for objectivity. Reflection enables us to begin to dis-identify from our instinctual nature and have a relationship to it rather than be utterly immersed within it. We begin to think about it, to bring understanding around it and the potential for greater communication. In our psychological journey this reflection is an important part of waking up to how we are, what motivates us and what our basic drives and needs are. It enables us to begin to live with them more consciously and in a healthier way that does not deny our natural instincts but rather integrates them with awareness.

The Preta Realm

Moving to the realm of the *pretas* or hungry ghosts, we encounter beings in a deep state of distress, characterised especially by intense craving. In this realm there is a longing for something to satisfy this craving and yet whatever is found does not come close to bringing satisfaction. This means that central to the pain and torment of the hungry ghost's inner reality is the agony of a continual search that will never bring relief or satisfaction.

While we may not believe in a literal hungry ghost realm, we almost certainly know something of this in our human condition when craving and dissatisfaction become unbearable. Our experience of this may be muted by the fact that we can keep finding things that *almost* satisfy this ache. The compulsive shopaholic, for example, is always looking for the next purchase to get some momentary glimpse of satisfaction, only for it to slip away. Our consumer culture stimulates this side of our nature by continually presenting us with better models, new fashions, latest upgrades and greater choice. We are the victims of this culture, and especially so if we have an inner hungry ghost.

Psychologically we could say that the root of the hungry ghost in us is a fundamental lack of nourishment of our sense of self in early infancy. Love and safe maternal holding is the foundation of healthy growth of our sense of self. When this basic need is not met we are left with a sense of inner hunger, yearning, pain and longing for something to satisfy it. Like the nourishment of mother's milk in infancy, this love is basic to our sense of well-being, and when we do not receive it or it is tainted by primary emotional distress, this lack leaves us hungry. It is the hungry ghost in us that may be like a desperately needy child never finding satisfaction. When this dominates our life, it can lead to a tortured, wretched, addictive, compulsive hunger that cannot be satisfied.

In this realm, Chenrezig appears as a monk sometimes carrying food and sometimes holding a vase of nectar.

Normally it is said that even if the hungry ghost finds food, it immediately turns to acid and does not satisfy. However, the food given by Chenrezig, the bodhisattva of loving kindness and compassion, offers the hungry ghost the potential to satisfy their hunger. The nectar is a gift of love that nourishes and satisfies as nothing else can and enables the hungry ghost's mind to begin to emerge from the wretchedness and torment they are in. Psychologically the suffering of our inner hungry ghost is only satisfied by the presence of love and careful, nourishing holding. If we can receive this, our mind may begin to emerge to an awareness that there is life beyond insatiable hunger.

The Narak Realm

In the next realm we encounter even greater torment. The *narak* realm of beings in hell is inhabited by those tormented as a result of their harmful, callous actions motivated by fear, hatred, anger and aggression. In the classical teachings on this realm, the suffering of these beings is vividly described in gruesome detail. This realm is reminiscent of many of the depictions of the hells in medieval Christian art, the works of Milton, Hieronymus Bosch and others. The Tibetans describe images of people tortured by so-called hell beings, their bodies cut and burned in horrific ways. Apart from the actual physical pain of this realm, the primary psychological characteristics are that those in this realm are full of hatred, fear and paranoia that projects a horrific reality. The experience of this state is such that a short time will feel like an eternity.

When we view this realm more as a state of being within the human condition, it is a very contracted, narrow state of mind tormented by hatred, aggression, bitterness and blame. This tormented mind projects a world of fear and paranoia, and these projections turn into the tormentors of a hellish world. I have seen this in people with severe mental illness such as a psychosis or schizophrenia, where distortions of reality can lead to fear and paranoia as though these people are being tortured and tormented by others around them. Anyone who has been through intense periods of depression will also know the distortion of time that can feel like an eternity of pain and despair. In this realm we lose all relationship to "reality" and live in a hallucinated world that is filled with distortions and projections of horrors. It is easy to see why it is said that a being in this world has no inner space for anything other than pain and torment. There is no possibility of any other kind of awareness. Although this could be said of the animal and preta realms as well, in this particular realm the hallucinated reality is incredibly powerful.

In this realm the compassionate presence of Chenrezig is sometimes described carrying a soothing balm, and at other times holding a flame. The soothing balm could be seen as an obvious manifestation of compassion that gives a sense of peace to a mind and body in such pain and anguish. Only when the pain diminishes will it be possible to begin to see through the distorted reality. Chenrezig holding a flame is interesting as it reflects what is being experienced. This reminds me of the role of the therapist who is there to simply reflect or mirror with compassion the pain that a client is in. Merely witnessing someone in the midst of such torment is a gift of compassion. I recall many years ago hearing how a well-known psychiatrist called R.D. Laing was said to work with schizophrenic patients. His way of working was to try and enter into their reality in order to really be able to empathise with and understand the distortion they experienced. When he saw the world as they did, he could support them to begin to make sense of it and slowly emerge. Chenrezig holding the flame can also symbolise the presence of someone who can lead those in hell out of the underworld. The flame brings light and illumination, awareness on the path towards health and liberation.

The Human Realm

Finally, we come to the human realm itself, usually considered the realm between the demi-gods and the animals. In discussing the previous five realms I have wanted to convey that we can recognise these five states of being within the human condition. What, then, makes the specifically human realm significant? The human realm is described as a state characterised by desire. This is not the extreme craving hunger of the preta realm. Here, desire is considered to be the root of human life and human endeavour. Sometimes this desire is seen as something wholly unwholesome, leading to endless craving and grasping. But desire can also be seen as that movement towards something that we seek to attain or achieve even on the spiritual path. In the human realm of desire there can be insatiable craving for things that will satisfy us, but what differentiates this from the preta is that humans have a great capacity to respond to that desire in creative ways which do bring some level of satisfaction. We are exceptionally clever, creative, enterprising and sophisticated in finding ways to achieve our aims and desires in order to temporarily satisfy ourselves. Unfortunately, this creativity and sophistication also leads to the relentless movement of the world of consumerism, of constantly changing fashion and endless striving for material gain. We are continually being seduced by advertising and so-called consumer choice to get the latest, most advanced possessions.

Human desire is an extraordinary motivating factor for both good and ill. It could be seen as a great gift leading to all the creative richness of our human world, from the arts to music to science and technology. We could say that the whole process of the advancement of the human experience is rooted in desire – but equally so its potential destruction. We consume and consume and have done so for thousands of years to the point today where our existence upon this planet is at risk.

Within our human condition there is also a very different, valuable expression of desire. The desire to gain knowledge may be part of this, but perhaps not necessarily the most beneficial part. More importantly, within our human capacity is the desire to gain understanding and awareness as well as the desire to care for and benefit others. The aspiration to attain liberation within the Buddhist world can equally be seen as a human capacity that emerges from desire.

In the human realm of the wheel of life, Chenrezig appears as a golden saffron-robed figure in a form that carries two objects. One is a begging bowl; the other is a staff adorned with three rings. The begging bowl is significant on several levels. It is a reflection of the monk who, having abandoned attachment and desire, becomes a wandering mendicant trusting in the kindness of others to provide food through donations to a beggar. This is an act of surrender that recognises the futility of continually being bound by worldly desire. But the begging bowl could also be seen as an acknowledgement of that very desire at the heart of our human condition. We cannot live without sustenance, and it is our desire that also sustains us. The monk surrenders to this reality and entrusts its fulfilment without grasping.

The staff that Chenrezig holds is known in Sanskrit as a *khakkhara*, or "sounding staff", which can have three, four or even six rings on it. It is said to be carried by a monk due to a wish to not harm others. As the monk walks, the sound of the rings gives warning to any creature in the environment of the monk's passing to scare away small insects and large prey. This helps the monk avoid inadvertently harming creatures as he walks. It is also sometimes said to notify any within earshot that the monk is there to receive alms. The sound of the rings on the staff could be seen as waking up and bringing awareness to all that come into relationship with the monk.

Within the human realm, Chenrezig is demonstrating the path that leads to awakening symbolised by the monk's staff. The human realm is often considered the one realm where the conditions for awakening are most present; the minds of those in this realm are most ready to be guided to liberation from suffering. Of all the realms, this is the one that has the least potential obstruction and its inhabitants can most readily become aware of the nature of our innate buddha potential.

In the teachings known as the graduated path to liberation, or *lam rim*, great emphasis is placed upon what is seen as the "precious human rebirth". This rebirth is endowed with great freedom to awaken. We can see from these six realms of existence that merely being born within a human form does not necessarily imply that we are inhabiting the human realm at all times. There are many periods in our life when we may recognise we are bound up in one of the other states and unable to truly manifest our human potential. When we practice the recitation of

the mantra of Chenrezig, we are potentially purifying the
seed causes of these six realms as they dwell in our nature.

4

The Origins of Suffering

W E HAVE SEEN how the mantra of Chenrezig brings us into relationship with the nature of suffering experienced within the six realms described in Buddhist teachings. Returning to our human condition, I would like to begin to look at the origins of our suffering particularly from a Western psychological viewpoint alongside a Buddhist understanding. This can help us to see why Chenrezig and his quality of compassionate presence is so significant in a healing process.

Within Buddhist teachings there is no developmental map of the psychological growth of the individual, from the time of conception, in the way that there is in contemporary Western psychology. In my own exploration of the convergence of Buddhism and Western psychotherapy I have found the Western understanding of the developmental process incredibly helpful. It gives us an insight into the roots of our complex psychological and emotional nature and how that shapes the unfolding of our life. We can begin to recognise the psychological origins of our suffering within this life as well as what may enable healing.

From the time of conception, in the womb and following birth, the environment within which we are born shapes our emerging sense of self. A Buddhist perspective, on the other hand, would also consider that we each bring with us into conception, from previous lives, a predisposition or susceptibility to respond to this environment. When this karmic predisposition comes into relationship with the environment of the womb and the presence of the mother, this interaction begins to form the emerging self. Through the womb into infancy, early childhood, school and other social contexts we are experiencing environments that are continually impacting and shaping our growing sense of self on a psychological and emotional level. How we respond to this process unfolding is very individual and depends on our susceptibility. But by the time we become adults we have all manner of emotional patterns and wounds that have become increasingly embedded in our being.

While much of our understanding of primary emotional patterning is oriented around the relationship to the mother, she is clearly only a small part of what shapes us as we grow. Still, the person who becomes our mother or primary care giver has to bear a huge responsibility for what it may mean to be a stable, healthy, caring and nurturing presence in the life of the growing fetus and infant. This archetypal demand for a mother placed upon the fallible human being that is our actual parent means it is no surprise that for many of us she inevitably falls short. Jung once wrote:

> This is the mother-love which is one of the
> most moving and unforgettable memories
> of our lives, the mysterious root of all
> growth and change; the love that means
> homecoming, shelter and the long silence
> from which everything begins and in which
> everything ends...but a sensitive person
> cannot in all fairness load that enormous
> burden of meaning, responsibility, duty,
> heaven and hell, on to the shoulders of one
> frail and fallible human being – so
> deserving   of   love,   indulgence,
> understanding and forgiveness – who was
> our mother.[7]

If we are fortunate, we will have experienced what has become known as the "good enough mother"[8]. If not, then we may have experienced, to some degree, the negative impact of the maternal environment. While once it was considered that the sense of self began to emerge after birth, it is now clear that there is an emergent self even within the womb that is affected by this environment.[9] In the therapeutic context, working with this level of experience is now much more familiar.

Following conception, our nascent sense of becoming is embedded in our mother's presence. She is the embodied expression of what we might call the *mother ground* as the source of our life. In his seminal book *The Ego and the Dynamic Ground*, Michael Washburn [10] sees this mother ground as a convergence of both an archetypal aspect of the "Great Mother" and a very human one. While the archetypal aspect is a dynamic, creative source imbued with huge potency, the human factor is understandably limited and fallible. Washburn called this original source the *Dynamic Ground* in which we are embedded from the moment of conception and from which we need to gradually emerge as our sense of self grows.

Our early experience of this mother ground will begin to colour and shape how our sense of self, the ego, begins to emerge. Ideally this ground offers a safe holding environment that enables us to rest in a profoundly settled, ecstatic sense of being. If our mother ground has been unstable, for whatever reason, it will lead to varying degrees of disturbance in the growing sense of our being or becoming. We could understand this relationship between our nascent sense of self and mother ground as like a seed within the soil. If the soil is moist and nutritious, the seed can be supported to grow healthily. If the soil is rocky and full of chemicals, the seed may struggle to grow. Because this mother ground is so charged with significance as the archetypal *ground of being*, the experience of some level of disruption can be profoundly impactful on the growing fetus and infant, and onwards into our life. As we will see later, this also has an impact on our capacity to rest deeply into states of meditation.

This experience of the early environment does not have to imply that the mother or primary care giver has intended to be destructive or harmful. For some of us this process may have been relatively undramatic, but still our sensitivity and innate propensity can mean we are deeply affected. The mere fact of our mother being a separate individual with her own emotional and psychological life impacts a sensitive child. Subtle nuances and changes in the maternal environment will be picked up and internalised to become elements shaping our sense of self. If the mother is anxious, upset or depressed, a sensitive infant feels it. If there are more serious disruptions to that early environment, such as parental conflicts, strong emotional volatility or some form of abuse, it can bring about much more deeply rooted feelings of insecurity, anxiety and a lack of safety. Then the experience of our *ground of being* becomes fractured, unstable and unsafe. Core emotional patterns of trauma become ingrained in our nature and colour our sense of self as we grow into our life. These patterns affect the way we subsequently relate to the world and how we believe it will respond to us. They will also be significant in how we engage in our relationships and in how our life unfolds.

These experiences can lead to the feeling that there is not a stable ground into which we can settle and feel safe to simply *be*. This can become compounded by the tendency we have as children to feel that this outer dysfunction must be because there is something wrong with us. We begin to believe that we are not accepted, not wanted, not good enough or ultimately unlovable. These feelings are very subtle and are experienced first on a cellular level, not as a cognitive awareness.

In my work as a psychotherapist as well as a spiritual mentor and Buddhist teacher, it has been clear how most of us suffer, to some degree, a wounded and insecure sense of self. The most familiar manifestation of this wounding is a fear that we are not good enough, that we are unloved, unwanted and so on. These painful feelings form a backdrop as we become more self-conscious, and our capacity for self-judgement and self-recrimination can also become more pronounced. It is as though we place upon our initial wounding a second layer of self-recrimination and criticism, accompanied by a persistent lack of self-acceptance and self-value. Our relationship to ourselves is then troubled and uncomfortable, and we are unable rest at ease in a deeper, healthy sense of being essentially OK.

This inner reality may be very familiar to many of us. We can learn to ignore or deny its presence; people who are highly functional in the world can often still have a wounded sense of self. We can cultivate all manner of ways of compensating for this lack, burying our wounding beneath carefully fabricated patterns of defence that, to the outside world, look relatively healthy. Many in our society who have achieved great things have done so as compensation for a deeper lack of self-value, self-love and self-acceptance. Our constant need to achieve and grow and our striving for excellence and material success are often a compensation for childhood wounds.

In the search for a sense of self-value and self-worth, the things we achieve in our lives and the satisfaction and recognition they bring can provide some sense of affirmation. The hazard remains that our sense of self is still vulnerable and can crumble when things go wrong, we are criticised, or our achievements are dismissed or not recognised. If there is not a deeper sense of secure emotional ground this can be very painful.

Our self-identity is surprisingly vulnerable and fragile if we have suffered early wounding or trauma. For many of us the capacity to suppress, overlook or deny it does not seem to be helpful; it does not go away. Those of us who become involved in spiritual practices such as Buddhism may feel that we are growing or developing "spiritually", but if our underlying wounding is not addressed, spiritual attainments are somewhat hollow. Regrettably, as is clear from people I have worked with over the years, many within the Buddhist world who have accomplished great amounts of study and even many meditation retreats still have unresolved psychological wounds. We can easily place a veneer of apparent spiritual attainment over our wounding but still it does not go away.

Much of our suffering is due to a fundamental lack of self-acceptance and self-value often accompanied by a harsh inner critical voice that continually harasses us. But this, in turn, is a reflection of a deeper absence of a stable ground of being that feels safe, compassionate, loving and accepting. This is the mother ground that could potentially have given us the inner ease to allow ourselves to restfully just be who we are, as we are. Some people have not suffered greatly in this way, but we almost all do to some degree – even though we may not yet be willing or able to recognise this in ourselves. When we are ready to begin to heal this wounding, our Buddhist practices can help if we know how to apply them skilfully. This requires that we allow ourselves to reconnect to the painful feelings that are there in the background of our experience and hold them with a sense of kindness and compassion. We need to relate to them with care and sensitivity, not with judgement, recrimination, shame or resentment. If we can begin to find a safe, compassionate holding environment to do this work, our capacity to tolerate and potentially heal this wounding can be strengthened and healing can begin. In this respect the compassionate presence of Chenrezig can be an extraordinary resource as a means of healing. Towards the end of this book I will introduce practices associated with Chenrezig that can enable us to feel a quality of compassionate presence to create a healing environment for this process to unfold.

5

Restlessness of Being

I N THE PREVIOUS CHAPTER I described a way in which we can understand the psychological roots of much of the wounding to our sense of self that affected us as we came into this life. One root is our relationship to the *ground of being* echoed by our experience of mother; the other is the emerging sense of self that grows within that holding context. I wish to add to this understanding something that is also seen as the root of suffering from a Buddhist perspective. The Buddha taught that *grasping*, in Tibetan *dochak*, is a fundamental disposition in our nature that is the cause of suffering. When we consider this from a more psychological perspective as an inner experience, I prefer to use the term *contraction*, because this is how it is usually felt, particularly in the body. The effect of this contraction is that we do not allow our natural emotional processes to remain fluid and pass though. As I have explained in some depth in *Feeling Wisdom*, it is not so much our emotions and feelings that are the problem, but how we respond to them. Our tendency is to tighten and solidify our experiences of pain and emotional distress, creating what might be seen as "packages" of trauma that remain held in the body. Modern psychotherapists such as Peter Levine[11], working in the world of trauma, consider the central problem to be that we tend to freeze around our experiences in order to cope with them. These psychotherapists are particularly referring to severe shock and trauma that becomes frozen in the body as the result of experiences such as abuse. Most of us, hopefully, do not experience anything as extreme; even so, we all suffer to some degree from the disposition to contract around our experiences, leading to a solidification of our sense of self.

In Buddhism, this disposition to contract and solidify our emotional experience is seen as the root of our suffering. At the heart of this is the tendency called in Tibetan *dakdsin*, ego-grasping, that contracts around an apparently solid, enduring, self-existent sense of "me". This contracted sense of self clings to an idea or a feeling about ourselves as something that is true and permanent. It *feels* as though it has a definite enduring reality, when in fact there is nothing substantial or enduring in the continual stream of our being. As is often said in the Buddhist world, we may wish to be free of suffering – but because of this ego-grasping we continually create its causes.

For most of us this solidified or contracted sense of "me" is not continually apparent but will manifest when some experience activates it. Then it will arise "vividly" and will often be accompanied by strong feelings that, as I suggest in the previous chapter, have become embedded in us from our early experiences of life. This is our wounded sense of self that becomes a deep source of suffering and can pervade our lives and motivate much of what we do. We may hold feelings such as "I am not good enough", "I am unacceptable", "I am bad, unlovable, unwanted, unsafe", and so on, in a way that makes them feel completely true, fixed and unchangeable. From these arise all kinds of emotional reactions that can reinforce the feelings even more. These emotional patterns become habitual and circular, not really resolving the discomfort. With this tendency it is very difficult to see the possibility that we could be different or to see that our self-beliefs are a distortion of reality. We are left with a powerful disposition to hold the sense of me to be true, enduring and self-existent. We do not see that our sense of self is just a process unfolding.

If we begin to look at the implications of the contraction around the sense of self, we see some significant consequences. Of particular interest is how it gives rise to a subtle existential suffering I like to call a *restlessness of being*. This is something we all experience deeply, but we do not necessarily recognise its presence until we stop and turn inwards. What becomes noticeable is that there is a subtle level of restlessness that is not really letting us relax and just "be". Instead we are always restlessly, busy *doing* in order to have a sense of being OK. Our culture is built around this wound, and the entire consumer industry could not flourish without constantly feeding on the roots of our suffering.

So long as we instinctively contract around a sense of self as something substantial and enduring, this restlessness will be there. It will be accompanied by a very subtle and very deep level of uncertainty and insecurity about our existence. This may be something that is just outside our field of awareness until we stop and attempt to relax or quieten. Then we may touch into an underlying restlessness that is always searching for something to engage with, or to do.

The emotional tone that accompanies this habit of ego-grasping will be a subtle level of anxiety, an existential anxiety at the heart of our restlessness of being. Because of it our ego will always need to find a way to create a sense of solidity, and so its disposition will be a restless movement into activity and form, into doing rather than being. Basically, so long as we can find something to relate to or do, then we will at least feel we exist. It often doesn't matter whether what we find to relate to is pleasant or unpleasant, the main thing is that we exist. Stephen Batchelor once called this habit of movement into form, "existential flight".[12]

There is a further significant aspect to our wounded ego: it is incredibly sensitive. Like a raw wound, it can easily feel hurt, criticized, victimised, abandoned, unsafe, unloved and so on, depending on the nature of the wound. This sensitivity can be unbearable and will often lead to a painful self-deprecating collapse on the one hand or a strong, angry, defensive reaction on the other. Either way, the ego's sensitivity to the impact of relationships in the world around can be acute and extremely painful.

It is important to consider at this point, when we recognise this disposition of ego-grasping and its associated anxiety and sensitivity, that we do need an ego. There has been a misconceived view sometimes amongst Buddhists that we do not need an ego and that it is the *problem*. From both a Buddhist and a psychological perspective this misses the point. Without an ego we cannot function in the world. Psychologically we would go into some form of fragmented psychosis. Having an ego is to have a functional focus of our relative ordinary sense of self in the world. This is not the same as ego-grasping where we contract into a wounded sense of self as solid and enduring. Our relative self is merely a process unfolding with a focus of attention that stabilises our identity.

Psychologically this restlessness of being particularly arises from disruptions in our very early experience of mother ground, our *ground of being*. This may begin in the womb as a holding environment and then extend to our world after birth. As I described in the previous chapter, our mother or primary care giver is the environment in which our nascent sense of self began to emerge. If this environment was emotionally safe, we may have felt a good enough a sense of trust that allowed us to relax, feel held, rest and let go into just *being*. If it was less than safe, it would have been a source of insecurity, anxiety and restlessness and we would not be able to settle deeply into a secure sense of being. An insecure ground means we do not feel safe to let go and open; instead it leads us to contract and tighten into a solid sense of self. It is important to recognise that, even with a relatively safe holding environment in our early life, the subtle tendency to contract around a sense of self will still be there as an instinctual ego-grasping. The difference will be the degree of emotional wounding that is present in the contracted nature of the self.

Perhaps unsurprisingly, our contracted sense of self is not comfortable with space even though we may yearn for it. We may instinctively seek a sense of safety and holding that could enable us to begin to relax, let go and just be. But this safety is very illusive and not something we are able to find in much of our world today. Sadly, because we cannot find it, we resort to all manner of sophisticated strategies, compensations and anaesthetics to help us cope.

For many of us our entry into the world of meditation appears to offer us a way of addressing some of our restlessness of being. With the right approach to meditation we can begin to relax, settle and touch into an inner quiet and stillness that can be deeply satisfying. In the tradition of mahamudra, which I will say more about later, we begin with the understanding that our mind's innate nature is essentially pure, spacious, clear awareness, free of confusion and emotional entanglement. This pristine nature of mind is often referred to as the *ground of being*, and it is significant that this ground in Buddhism is also associated with the mother. It is *mother clear-light* or the *ocean of dharmakaya* associated with the Great Mother and it has a parallel in Washburn's "dynamic ground". This is our innate nature, within us from the moment of conception, yet veiled and obscured by our emotional patterning and restlessness that arises from our contracted sense of self.

In the practice of mahamudra meditation we begin to restore our relationship to the ground of being, the innate spacious and empty nature of awareness. The process of meditation, however, is not easy. We will encounter times when we meet barriers of resistance to letting go and opening. These barriers can be a subtle – or sometimes not so subtle – restlessness, anxiety and tension that simply does not allow us to settle, let go and open. It is as though on some very deep, almost instinctual level we do not feel it is safe to let go, open and drop into the ground of being. This is in part because within spacious awareness our contracted self has no basis to abide. As a consequence, our ego kicks in with its natural mechanism of self-protection. We may even feel that the ground of being is like an abyss into which we will fall and be annihilated. It has become the dark terrible mother. We are encountering a return to the same fear and contraction that may have been there in our earlier life when, on some very deep primal level, we did not feel our mother ground was safe.

This is not wrong or bad, it simply means that we are reconnecting to our inner reality with the potential to enable it to heal.

Central to this entire process will be our relationship to the body. The restlessness of being in our nervous system is felt in the body. The contraction around our sense of self and the anxiety that accompanies it will be felt in the body. It is unfortunate that, in the West, all of these "symptoms" at the root of our restlessness of being have led many of us to become more disconnected from the body. The most common consequence is that we can become stuck in our heads, with persistent restless mental chatter the Tibetans call *namtok*. If we are to truly relax into the potential depth of our being, this intellectual mental process has to quieten so that we have a chance to settle back into the body. This is where we will come back into relationship with the existential nature of our restlessness and its underlying emotional tone of anxiety.

In meditation, as we encounter layers of contraction, it requires a repeated process of letting go, relaxing and opening. What supports this is the presence of a compassionate holding environment that allows us to feel safe enough to begin to let go and open to what we feel. The presence of a healthy quality of compassionate acceptance is like the loving parent that enables us to really begin to settle and let go. It is a quality of acceptance and kindness that can allow all of our early painful feelings to arise and move through thanks to a sense of safety. In the practice of Chenrezig we begin to meet an expression of that compassionate presence, embodying a quality of unconditional love and kindness that we can potentially feel as a safe healing presence. In this compassionate presence we can begin to relax our contracted nature and open to our inner sense of spaciousness, fluidity and simply being.

6

Chenrezig and Compassionate Presence

WHEN WE COME into an environment or a relationship that feels safe and compassionate, it can feel like a safe enough context for some of the wounding and pain we have buried to come to the surface to be healed. Bringing the compassionate presence of Chenrezig into our awareness through our meditation practice can begin to create a safe environment for this healing to happen. Significantly, within the context of retreats I have led where Chenrezig is the central holding presence, I have often seen this process begin. As people allow themselves to be held in his compassionate presence, rather than feeling a wonderful, peaceful emotion-free experience as they might expect, instead they find that their pain and trauma start to come to the surface. I often find myself needing to reassure them that this is not bad or wrong. It is reflection of the way in which to heal; we need a safe, free and secure compassionate space that will allow what has been held in and suppressed to start to emerge.

To me, as a psychotherapist, this experience is very familiar. When a client begins to feel truly safe and held, then it is possible to allow feelings to come awake that may have been long buried. There is an interesting reality to the way in which we tend to bury what we cannot cope with because there is not a safe environment to process it. This is not a bad thing; it is a natural aspect of our capacity to survive. In the same way, a child that has suffered abuse in some way finds a way to bury it deep within in order to survive. The pain can remain buried and will not heal until an environment that is safe and compassionate allows it to begin to resurface. Much of psychotherapeutic work is around creating a free and secure, safe environment for a client, to enable and allow whatever needs to emerge to gradually come into the light of day and begin to be healed. I say healed – but this is not exactly the correct word if we think that healing implies that it is all gone away. What the healing process can do, however, is to enable us to begin to digest and integrate what has happened in a more healthy way. To be able to tolerate feelings that were intolerable and enable them to begin to release and be less charged. We will inevitably be changed by the process, but aspects of our pain may still remain as echoes of what we have been through. They shape who we are.

What enables healing is compassionate presence. The presence of Chenrezig can begin to offer that for our own experience of suffering and then also enable us to become a resource for the healing of others. In chapters 4 and 5, I was describing two particular dimensions of our suffering that are helped by the quality of compassionate presence that Chenrezig embodies. When we suffer from a wounded sense of self that leads us to feel we are abandoned, unloved or not good enough, we need the presence of compassion that is there for us without judgement and agendas. If we work within the practice of Chenrezig, there is a way in which we can begin to receive his *blessing* as an unconditional compassionate presence. The term "blessing" in Tibetan is *jinlab*, sometimes translated as "waves of inspiring strength", implying that his presence brings an energy that is nourishing and encouraging. As I have suggested in chapter 1 regarding the qualities of the form of Chenrezig, he sits in a posture that expresses a number of significant things. His posture is balanced and centred, suggesting a sense of equanimity that is steady and free of biases and judgements. He is undisturbed by our struggles. He does not give us the feeling that our experiencing these struggles means that there is something wrong with us.

Compassion is not about having to be perfect or live up to ideals we measure ourselves by. Self-compassion is a genuine care and kindness towards ourselves as we are, with all of our faults, pain and difficulties as well as our qualities and talents. It is unfortunate that many of us do not grow up with a particularly compassionate presence as part of our outer environment; as a result we inevitably do not have a compassionate inner environment.

With clients I have seen over the years, it has often been painfully apparent how much they lacked that presence of unconditional compassion. Instead there is a kind of harshness in their inner world that comes out in the therapy space. It can feel cold, uncaring and potentially disapproving and full of critical voices that seem hard to dispel. They may be in deep pain and yet this pain is compounded by the further imposition of a feeling that this is bad, wrong or shameful. I notice that, if I can genuinely bring a sense of compassionate presence when holding the therapeutic space, then something relaxes in the client. It is as though the safety of a compassionate space that does not judge them gives permission for what is painful to be felt and allowed to begin to transform. To me as a therapist, the quality of Chenrezig has always felt significant, and I have often spent some time bringing his presence into the space either before or during a session.

When we can be in the presence of someone who holds us with compassion, we can also begin to find the capacity for compassion towards ourselves. We can allow ourselves more kindness around our pain and more space to be who we are. In our meditation, the presence of Chenrezig can bring a deep healing to our sense of self if we allow ourselves to open and receive his loving compassionate energy. When in the front-generation practice (see chapter 9) we bring Chenrezig into our awareness in the space before us, we should not think of this as just something we imagine as a visualisation. We need to gradually open to the felt sense of his quality, his energetic nature, as a real presence. If we can do that and allow a sense of intimacy in receiving that presence, it can have a profound effect. To do this we need to remember that he is an emanation of our essential buddha-nature, inseparable from all the buddhas. His nature is the energy of sambhogakaya and we need to give ourselves time to feel this presence, allowing it to wash down through us in the form of light energy.

Not only can this relationship to Chenrezig begin to heal our wounded sense of self; it will also have a deeper effect on our experience of the *restlessness of being*. This restlessness – one of the primary symptoms of the contraction around our sense of self that is the root of our suffering – is often accompanied by a subtle level of anxiety that cannot let go and relax into a more spacious ground of being. The contracted sense of self, *ego-grasping*, can be addressed on one level through the realisation of the empty nature of the ego. But this is not always such an easy realisation to gain because it tends to be a conceptual understanding not easily translated into direct experience. The experience of a safe, compassionate, accepting environment, however, can begin to soften and loosen the contraction. If we create an inner environment that is open, allowing and compassionate, then we will be able to begin to relax and settle into a deeper sense of ease and restfulness of being. Our contracted sense of self can then begin to soften and open because it feels a growing sense of safety and greater comfort resting in space.

Meditations that begin to create a spacious, compassionate sense of safety can be an antidote to the contracted restlessness deep in our nature. There are two particular approaches to meditation that can facilitate this. One is in relationship to Chenrezig and the other is the practice of mahamudra. Mahamudra is, as I have said, an approach to meditation that leads us to settle in open spacious awareness that is free of contraction. I have explored this in depth in *Tasting the Essence of Tantra* and I will explain in chapter 14 how our deity meditation within the tantric tradition needs to be grounded in the practice of mahamudra. In the practice of mahamudra, we begin by returning to an awareness of the body and the cultivation of a deep sense of relaxation and grounding. This in itself begins to create the conditions for the growing capacity to rest and settle in a more spacious and open awareness. This process naturally counters the contracted disposition that is so central to our restlessness of being. Our body is bound up in this contracted tendency on a cellular level and, when our awareness becomes quieter and more open, we may start to recognise it. This gives us the potential to naturally release and soften the habitual tendency of contraction around our sense of self, allowing it to become more fluid and permeable. We are also countering our restlessness because we are becoming more and more comfortable resting in space rather than being caught in anxiety that solidifies our sense of self. Although this approach is not a conceptual understanding of the emptiness of self, it is a more direct way of enabling the disposition deeply embedded in our body to change and open.

Because the cause of suffering is contraction, the combination of Chenrezig's compassionate presence with the capacity to rest in that spacious openness of awareness has a profound effect on our wounded sense of self as well as the underlying restlessness of being. Over the many years I have taught this approach in retreats, people have often responded with a real appreciation for its effectiveness.

7

Tonglen and the Inner Child

ONE WAY OF RECOGNISING the root of suffering in ourselves is to relate to it as our own inner wounded child. Although this has become something of a cliché in the psychotherapy world, that does not diminish its value as a way of understanding ourselves better. In the therapy context it is very common to find that someone who gets in touch with some of the deeper sense of wounding to self-value and self-identity has the feeling of being very young. When something occurs that puts us in touch with that vulnerability, we will often immediately feel younger. The age that we are taken back to may vary depending on what has particularly been touched; we may find we have a spectrum of child aspects that vary in age and have different characteristics depending upon that age. The way we may have felt as a seven-year-old has a different quality and different memory to when we were a teenager or in puberty. Sometimes when our emotional life is stimulated it takes us back to very early preverbal and even prenatal experiences that are still present, and that can bring feelings of anxiety, abandonment and lack of a safe, loving environment.

This can mean that we need to begin to relate to this child aspect of ourselves more consciously to discover what is being held by that experience. To do this, however, may not be easy because it can put us in touch with extremely painful feelings, memories and even trauma in the past. It is not uncommon for us to feel reticent to allow the feelings of this child, especially if we see it as needy or unacceptable. Some of us may have a very conscious dislike of this inner child, or feel ashamed of it, and would not want the world to know of its presence. It becomes an aspect of our shadow that is not revealed. Nevertheless, our relationship to this part of us is very significant. If we are living with feelings of insecurity, lack of self-value or self-acceptance, then this anxious inner child is almost certainly going to be present in our shadow. Often a troubled or ambivalent relationship to our inner child contributes to painful feelings of shame, but if we can rectify and heal this relationship we will begin to feel very different.

If we struggle to recognise this aspect of ourselves, we need to notice how we respond in relationships where we feel emotionally triggered. Many of the arguments and feelings of hurt in relationships are a reflection of our inner child being activated. Getting to know this part of ourselves may be very beneficial in resolving our relationship problems. Healing it can also be extremely important in actually restoring a relationship to ourselves that has become broken in the course of our life. Several people I have worked with who have explored this process in the way I will describe have said that it restores a sense of the continuity of themselves, rather than feeling dislocated from their childhood. For others it has meant coming back to a place where they have seen that their feelings of aloneness, isolation or abandonment have actually been because they have been abandoning themselves on a deep level – they have been abandoning their own inner child because they felt ashamed and repelled by it.

It is also important to hold the process of healing with care and sensitivity. This part of us needs to be understood and accepted and then gradually given the space to be liberated from whatever pain it feels. As the trauma of the inner child begins to soften and heal, this can be a strong experience. Sometimes this needs careful therapeutic support, especially if there were shocking experiences that begin to re-awaken. The work of people such as Peter Levine[13] tells us that we need to awaken these experiences gradually and in a resourced way so that we do not re-traumatise ourselves by moving too fast with the process. The degree of wounding we may have suffered is not always immediately apparent because it is often relatively unconscious and held in the body. I cannot overemphasise the need for skilful professional support if we become aware that something begins to awaken that is particularly disturbing or hard to bear on our own. We all suffer some degree of wounding from childhood; for some of us, however, this may be more severe and need therapeutic help.

The way I am going to introduce healing the inner child relates to the practice of *tonglen* and is a relatively gentle process. It may bring up strong feelings but if we allow these to be as they are, with a quality of kindness and compassion, then they can move through and heal. The important thing is to not be afraid to feel what arises and to give it space to move through. This is something I have gone into in more depth in *Feeling Wisdom*.

We can use the practice of tonglen in relation to how we are in our current or recent life. However, since there has often been greater impact upon us in certain critical periods in childhood, tonglen practice with different aspects of ourselves in childhood can be particularly helpful. It is these times that we can come back to in meditation and take through a healing process. This may mean we can begin with a very small and young child and then slowly work forward to puberty, teens, adolescence and so on. Each of these phases may have some element of emotional distress and wounding. Often there is a compounding effect of later experiences having been laid upon earlier ones. They may also correspond to a particular point in life where some external condition or circumstance, like a change of school, a parental divorce, a new step-parent, an illness or bereavement, had a dramatic effect upon us.

In the practice of tonglen, *tong.pa*, in Tibetan, means "to give", and *len.pa* means "to take". Traditionally this refers to the way in which we cultivate compassion and love. When we cultivate compassion we consider taking on (*len.pa*) the suffering of others. When we cultivate love we give (*tong.pa*) happiness. This meditation is traditionally practiced by visualising another person or persons in front of us that we choose in order to develop a more loving and compassionate relationship. Here, however, I specifically wish to describe visualising ourselves in front as the object of meditation, but as we were as a child. To make this most effective it may be worth reflecting before the meditation on what particular time of your life you wish to explore. An example of this meditation could be as follows:

*****

To begin this meditation, spend some time settling and resting into the body, quietening your mind. After a while imagine the presence of Chenrezig in the heart chakra. Find a suitable size – not too big nor too small. He is seated in his usual form upon a lotus and moon disc, white in colour with four arms, surrounded by an aura of light. Spend a while resting with this awareness of Chenrezig in the heart.

Then bring your child-self into the space before you and spend some time tuning into and reflecting upon the nature of your child's suffering. Be aware, if you can, of the circumstances that may have given rise to this suffering. Try not to become too caught in the story that may arise. Instead, notice what feelings this brings, allowing them to be there and letting them be free to move through. After some time, consider how you would like to take away the suffering, confusion and pain of your child. As you breathe in, imagine that you breathe in the suffering of "you" in front, in the form of grey smoke. Let this smoke come down into your heart where it touches Chenrezig and is instantly transformed into a light of compassion and love. As you continue, let this have the effect of melting and softening your heart and opening your connection to the child before you. Have the sense that your child-self begins to be released from its suffering.

After a while bring this in-breath to an end, rest for a short period and then begin to consider in what way you would like your inner child to be endowed with a sense of happiness, self-worth and joy. As you breathe out imagine that, from Chenrezig in your heart, a light of love and kindness goes out, opening your heart to a feeling of warmth and care. Let this continue for some time, gradually opening and softening your heart towards your inner child. Have the sense that this child feels lighter, nourished and satisfied by the light of love you have emanated.

Spend some time with the process of the in-breath and then the out-breath, giving enough time to deepen the experience. Finally, rest with the feelings that remain from this meditation and let them expand from your heart and spread through your body. Stay with this for as long as you can so that you really relax in the feeling, allowing yourself to digest what may have arisen. Following this, it can be good to spend a short while whispering the mantra of Chenrezig, emanating light of compassion and love from his heart, blessing the child. Then imagine that the child in front comes into the heart of Chenrezig in your heart. Again, rest with the felt experience of this for a while.

*****

What can be important with this meditation is to allow time to remain in touch with the feelings it brings up. If these are negative or painful feelings, then let them be as they are without judging them or pushing them away, and without contracting around them and holding on to them.

It is important to let these feelings pass through, as they will be part of the healing process. We cannot expect to begin to open our hearts and feel loving and positive without some of the feelings coming to the surface that were part of the closing down. When we do this meditation, we may feel a level of sadness, grief or anger. We may contact some of the feelings of a lack of self-worth or not being good enough that are part of our wounding. We may experience feelings of dislike or even hatred arising in relation to the child in front. Do not be disturbed by these feelings. Allow them to be as they are and give them space to arise and move through. Accept them and let them go. It is when we block and tighten around these feelings that they become stuck again; the intention of the meditation is to release and heal.

As these feelings begin to release and move through, there is the potential for a quality of love and compassion to emerge towards ourselves. When this arises, try to simply stay with those feelings and let them expand and fill you, softening and opening your heart. Take as much time as you need to remain with the feelings that grow before you move to the final stage of absorbing your child-self into your heart.

Doing the tonglen meditation in the way I have described can, over time, radically change our inner relationship. Whereas at one time we may have disliked or felt embarrassed or ashamed of this side of ourselves, gradually we can come to a more peaceful relationship. We should not underestimate the difference we can feel in ourselves when our inner child feels accepted, loved and held with compassion and understanding.

8

Cultivating Our Relationship

I HAVE WRITTEN at some length about the need to heal some of our early wounding, suggesting that possibly the most healing quality is that of compassionate presence. I have also described the way in which Chenrezig is seen as the buddha of compassion or what we might also call the bodhisattva of compassionate presence. It is this quality of compassionate presence that we definitely need to allow ourselves to feel as we begin to develop our relationship to Chenrezig.

When we practice the *front-generation* meditation we are starting to cultivate this healing relationship. This cultivation can have a deep significance because, as a compassionate presence, Chenrezig offers a quality of unconditional care and love that allows us to be as we are, free of judgement. This is the unconditional love and compassion we needed so much in childhood but may not have felt. It is the quality that can begin to allow us to relax and feel held so that we may slowly return to a sense of *restfulness* in our being.

In meditation the presence of Chenrezig can help us to rest more at ease in our body as we allow ourselves to receive his presence. The question may be whether we can actually allow ourselves to receive. Some of us may have difficulty with this because we are not sure we can trust and open. We may also not really believe he is actually a presence we can relate to rather than just something we invent or imagine. When we begin to do this kind of meditation we may have the sense that we are making this up. We are visualising and imagining him to be there – but not really, especially if we are not particularly good at visualisation. This doubt and uncertainty is understandable because we are not used to the idea that Chenrezig is an emanation of the buddhas and our own nature as a real presence. We are not simply visualising him; we are inviting his presence into the space. As we do the meditation of front-generation there is a process that opens a doorway, so to speak, to his presence. We create the conditions for this to happen and, as we do, we can increasingly *feel* Chenrezig's energetic quality in the space even if we are not good at visualising.

This experience is more likely if we can drop out of our conceptual mind and begin to settle into a quiet quality of clear awareness before we begin. As we do that, we create the inner conditions for Chenrezig to emerge as an expression of the nature of our mind – not just a conceptual fabrication. We can then feel in our body a deepening energetic felt sense of his quality.

When beginning the front-generation practice, following any initial refuge and bodhicitta prayers to create the intention for our practice, we need to spend time settling into meditation. This may begin with awareness within body sensation and feeling. This awareness gradually settles and opens to become more spacious. If you are used to the practice of mahamudra, this is a time when you need to bring that experience to the beginning of the deity process. This enables our practice to emerge or unfold within the context of the spacious clarity of awareness and emptiness. (I will explain the relationship between Chenrezig and mahamudra in more depth in chapter 14.)

Once we have settled into the space of awareness, in the space in front at the level of the forehead, we imagine there arises an eight-petalled white lotus and moon disc at the centre of which stands a syllable HRIH. The syllable HRIH is known as a seed syllable because it is the seed of light and sound from which the deity Chenrezig will come into being. The HRIH can be visualised within a white flame or, if the Sanskrit syllables are not easy to imagine, the flame will be sufficient. If combined, we imagine that standing in the middle of the moon disc is a white flame marked by a syllable HRIH at its centre. The flame and HRIH radiate light out into the space around. That light invites from dharmakaya the essence of all the buddhas' awakened compassion and love in the aspect of millions of tiny white Chenrezigs that absorb back into the flame. These Chenrezigs come from all directions, not just from above and around. They absorb into the flame, melting as though they are snowflakes. This imbues the flame and HRIH with powerful vibrant light energy so that it begins to blaze with light, eventually transforming into the aspect of Chenrezig. It is helpful to take time with this visualisation

HRIH

because this is a moment when we experience the gateway opening to the presence of Chenrezig. I use the term gateway as a metaphor for how, from dharmakaya, the energy of sambhogakaya begins to move into form. There is a kind of communication happening, from the awakened nature of dharmakaya through sambhogakaya into manifestation.

The flame and HRIH transform into the aspect of Chenrezig seated upon the lotus and moon disc before us. He has all the characteristics I have described in chapter 1. He is seated in the full lotus posture with one face and four arms, dressed in robes of silk and adorned with ornaments of gold and jewels. Chenrezig smiles with narrow, compassionate eyes like a loving parent for his only child and is surrounded by an aura of light. As we rest with an awareness of Chenrezig's presence, it is helpful to attune ourselves to the qualities he holds, reminding ourselves of his deeply compassionate nature that does not judge us and looks at us as a loving parent would.

At this point in our meditation, there are two things we can do to enhance our relationship to Chenrezig. One is to make prayers and the other is to make offerings. Formal, traditional prayers are often in the form of praises and acknowledgements of his qualities. We can also make much more personal prayers and ask for his blessings. I find this to be an important time of connection and opening; I begin to feel a kind of intimacy with his presence. I begin to open to his holding quality and in my heart I receive his energetic nature. Following these prayers, we can then also make the traditional offerings to the five senses; these are water for drinking and washing, followed by flowers, incense, lights, perfume, food and music. These will usually be offered using the appropriate mudras while holding a vajra and bell.

Following these prayers and offerings we imagine in Chenrezig's heart there is a moon disc upon which stands the syllable HRIH surrounded by the syllables of the mantra. Before we begin to recite or chant the mantra, it is helpful to spend a while allowing ourselves to tune in to Chenrezig's presence and become aware of light emanating from his heart into our heart and into our body. We need to let this light of compassion and love fill every atom of the body, bringing a deep sense of compassionate acceptance and well-being. After a while we begin to hear the sound of the mantra and, as we begin to chant or whisper the mantra on the breath (quietly mouthing the mantra), continue to receive his presence.

When we have recited the mantra for some time, we can stop the recitation and rest with the quality of spacious awareness that remains. I have explained this process at some length in *Tasting the Essence of Tantra*. Resting in that space of awareness, we will also experience a felt sense of the quality that Chenrezig begins to generate within our nervous system. We begin to feel a combination of compassionate presence with the natural spaciousness of awareness itself. This experience can transform us very deeply.

Once we have remained in spacious awareness for some time, we again restore our awareness of the radiant presence of Chenrezig in the space in front. He then comes to the crown of the head and, becoming smaller, descends into the heart, blessing our heart-mind. As this practice deepens, our relationship to Chenrezig as a holding presence and refuge becomes stronger. There can be a growing sense of intimacy in our relationship which can deepen as we move to the meditation where he is present in the heart (see chapter 12).

9

Healing the Heart

WITHIN THE TIBETAN TRADITION as well as many other spiritual traditions, the heart chakra is seen as an important centre of our being. In the path of tantra in particular, the heart chakra is often seen as the abode of our primordially pure buddha-nature and the source of significant qualities in our spiritual awakening. Bodhicitta is often seen as the *heart essence[14]*, the source of the vital energy of love, compassion and joy. Many practices within the tantric tradition begin from the heart chakra and eventually return to the heart.

Recognising that the energy within the heart chakra is so important, I was surprised when one of my Tibetan teachers said he thought that many of us in the West suffered from an impairment of the *soklung* or "life supporting wind". He went on to say that many of us seemed to have a kind of pain and contraction that was like a compression or closing off of the heart. He seemed surprised or even shocked at the degree of heart wounding he saw in many of us. I learned that this could be understood as the damage or blockage of the energy in the heart that particularly comes from excessive pressure in the heart. As I explored this further, it became clear to me that something about the Western culture in which we grow up has a detrimental impact upon the heart chakra. As Westerners, many of us grow up in a challenging and stressful social and cultural environment, and its impact gradually has a damaging effect on the heart chakra. From early on in our lives we are expected to function in a demanding, competitive, sometimes hostile world where we are required to become self-reliant, successful individuals. Our Western education system is incredibly demanding and stressful on young children; the incidence of depression is extremely high. It is no wonder that to survive – especially if we are sensitive – we learn to close our hearts to protect ourselves.

Our soklung being harmed leads to a lack of deep joy and openness and makes us feel a subtle sense of sadness or dissatisfaction about our lives. This can be felt as a mildly depressive feeling as though there is a hole that cannot be filled. We may learn to compensate for this by the countless sophisticated ways in which we try to fill the hole with material possessions, sensory pleasures and relationships, but they only touch the surface and do not address the core issue, a lack of relationship to our heart essence.

If we wish to begin to awaken within us the qualities of love, compassion and joy, we need to heal the wounding of the heart and restore our relationship to the source of our vitality. This is not to say that everyone's heart is completely closed, but we can all benefit from ways of enabling our heart to be more open and more responsive to others. If we wish to cultivate the quality of bodhicitta and wish to awaken to be of benefit to others, then this healing process is extremely important.

In the previous chapter I have described the process of front-generation in which we begin to cultivate a closer relationship to the presence of Chenrezig. It is within this meditation that we can start to explore healing what has closed the heart. To open our heart requires in part that we feel safely held within a loving, compassionate environment so that we can start to let go and relax. That safety may be created by a supportive retreat environment but is especially aided by an awareness of Chenrezig as a holding presence. Within the context of our relationship to the practice of Chenrezig, there is then great value in a particular orientation of meditation.

In the process of meditation, it is important to consider that we will almost certainly not experience an opening of the heart without feeling something of the pain that closed us down in the first place. This may be negative feelings towards ourselves. It may be feelings of sadness and despair at the experience of a lack of love. It may be that we return to the fear and hurt that caused us to close our heart in the first place. We cannot assume that we will experience wonderful blissful feelings of warmth, joy or love immediately. This is unrealistic and does not take into account the fact that opening the heart is a process; it takes time and careful practice. Most of all it requires that we are ready to soften and relax around the heart.

In the front-generation meditation I described in the previous chapter, we are cultivating a relationship to Chenrezig as an emanation of compassionate presence. Once you have settled into a closer feeling of his quality as I described, you can then begin a heart-healing meditation as follows:

*****

In the heart of Chenrezig is a moon disc with a small white syllable HRIH standing at its centre. Around this HRIH circle the syllables of the mantra OM MANI PADME HUNG. From the HRIH in Chenrezig's heart, a radiant white light begins to emanate. This is a warm white, not a cold white, and brings with it a sense of Chenrezig's compassion and love as a healing energy. It is important that, as much as you can, you let this energy of light and love touch your heart. As you breathe in, breathe that light into your heart, letting it begin to soften and open the heart. Have the sense that what was solid, stuck and frozen in the heart begins to melt so that you can receive more and more of Chenrezig's light energy. As you breathe out, let that light spread to every cell of your body, blessing your body, speech and mind. Feel that as your heart opens you are filled with the radiance of Chenrezig's blissful compassionate energy. Then, when you are ready, begin to introduce the sound of the mantra. This can be chanted or whispered depending upon what feels to be most effective. Once you have done this for some time, let the mantra cease, then rest in the space of awareness, giving particular attention to the subtle felt sense in the heart and the rest of the body. Allow that feeling to spread and open, becoming more spacious.

*****

We may need to spend a lot of time on this kind of meditation to soften and open our heart. This can be a gradual process that will pass through stages that may bring painful things to the surface. If this happens, allow those feelings space to move through; they are not wrong or bad. This meditation can also slowly awaken a warmth and love in the heart that naturally enables us to begin to open to others. I have found that it is worth following the breathing process I have described for as long as you feel it is necessary to start to have a sense of its effect before beginning to introduce the sound of the mantra.

10

Turning Towards Others

TURNING TOWARDS the suffering of others
becomes increasingly possible as we begin to heal our
own wounding and develop a greater sense of self-value
and self-compassion. So long as we are still caught up in
our own wounding, a level of self-preoccupation will make
it very difficult to truly engage with others' lives. The
Tibetans, unfortunately, like to call this self-preoccupation
"self-cherishing", an expression which I feel is very
unhelpful since many of us need to learn to love and
cherish ourselves to heal what is wounded. Regardless of
what we call it, healing our wounded sense of self is at the
root of our capacity to then turn towards others with love
and compassion. So long as we are still preoccupied by our
own suffering, or indeed with our own happiness, then we
will not have the inner space to open to others with any
degree of real empathy.

Our growing compassion for others requires that we
have the courage and openness to connect to and be

touched by their suffering. We need to allow ourselves to feel how it must be for someone else as they are going through difficulties and hardships. We may call this feeling empathy or sympathy; these are subtly different. Our empathy resonates with the feeling that someone is experiencing in a way that makes it very immediate and not always easy to bear. Our sympathy recognises the suffering someone is in even though we do not feel it so directly and intimately. It is from these two, however, that our compassion for the suffering we see around us can grow. We start to see that, even in our relatively comfortable Western lives, we still struggle emotionally in many ways. Despite the relative good fortune we may have on a material level, there is often so much psychological pain and suffering. When we open our awareness out into the wider world, however, we can see that there is so much fear and physical pain and insecurity. The global nature of our media makes this only too present in our awareness; we are constantly being reminded of where people's lives are wrecked by wars, terrorism, political and economic upheaval and natural disasters. If we truly allow ourselves to feel its impact, the scale of this may sometimes feel hard to bear. The damage being done to the planet can be equally devastating if we actually allow ourselves to open to its presence.

When we allow ourselves to be touched by the suffering we see around us, we then need to recognise that we are all alike in wishing to be free of suffering and to experience happiness. Whatever our colour, race, religion or socio-economic status, everyone wishes to be free of suffering and to experience happiness. The problem we see in the world is that we often do not truly understand what the causes for happiness are. Instead, out of ignorance, we create ever more causes for suffering. We could say that even a terrorist is motivated by this intention to be free of suffering and to experience happiness, just as much as a banker or a thief. When we understand this, it leads us to a sense of greater equanimity in our relationships. Despite any apparent social and economic differences, we are all in essence no different in what motivates our life. Upon this very simple recognition, compassion can naturally grow.

Once we recognise that we are all essentially motivated by the same intention to be free of suffering, it is helpful to open to the awareness that we are intimately interconnected with those who live on the planet with us. While this is not always obvious, it becomes so when we stop and consider the things in our life that arise because of the work and efforts of countless others. The fact that so much of what we use and consume in the West is produced in the Far East makes this realisation unavoidable. Some time ago I was looking to buy pieces of sandstone that could be used as paving in our garden. When I asked the woman in the store where they came from, she replied, "India". As soon as she said this I had a pang of uncertainty. How would I feel about this ethically? I became aware of the implications in terms of the living conditions of those who produced them. Having lived in India, I knew it would be produced in a way that almost certainly pays little regard for the safety and well-being of those who made it - yet it is through their suffering and hardship that it becomes possible for me in the West to enjoy these things.

As we develop our compassionate awareness towards others, a central ingredient must be a consideration for their welfare and how our actions impinge upon others. Consideration for others is such a simple thing but its significance is huge. It is a shift from a relatively narrow, self-oriented way of thinking to a much bigger view. Lama Yeshe would sometimes describe what he called a *big mind* in relation to how we open to and consider the lives of others. He was implying that it helps for us to place our own lives in relation to the suffering of others. Rather than being preoccupied by a small-minded disposition that thinks primarily of *my* life and *my* problems, we open to a bigger perspective. Seeing the pain and devastation in people's lives when there are natural disasters like earthquakes, tornadoes or raging wildfires puts my life into perspective. It makes my own difficulties seem somewhat insignificant. Not irrelevant, but less significant in the greater scheme of things.

Opening to the lives of others and their hardship and efforts is an important aspect of our development of compassion and, ultimately, the cultivation of bodhicitta. It makes us more connected in our shared humanity and the challenge of what it means to be alive. We all share this struggle for existence and, despite the so-called advances of our modern world, we do not seem to create much greater happiness. Perhaps today, with a global pandemic and an acute environmental crisis, things are even more difficult, more insecure and more stressful. When we put these into the context of the global consequence of our lives upon the planet, we need to have a sense of compassion for our human frailty as well as our human fallibility. We are extremely adept at perpetuating the causes of suffering and not so skilful at genuinely creating the causes for happiness.

Turning outwards to look at the suffering of the world around is not a comfortable process, but it is a necessary one if we are to find a compassionate relationship to the world that surrounds us. We can see this in our relationship to the creatures that inhabit the planet as well as to the planet itself. As we open ourselves to life in all its rawness and allow ourselves to feel, it is also helpful to begin to awaken the quality of bodhicitta in our hearts. As I have described in an earlier chapter, bodhicitta is the awakening mind or heart essence, a wish to fully awaken in order to free others from suffering. We may have a growing feeling of compassion, but we will often also have a sense of our limitation to truly be of help. What we discover from our understanding of Buddhism is that within us we all have the potential to awaken fully to our innate buddha-nature. It is through this awakening that we will ultimately be of greatest benefit to others. It will take us beyond our ordinary limitations and enable us to be able to liberate others from suffering.

11

Embodying Compassionate Presence

WITHIN the Tibetan Buddhist tradition, compassion is seen as an active intention that motivates us to want to liberate others from suffering. It is not sufficient to just *wish* others to be free of suffering, we need to actively engage in the process of helping others because their suffering is so immediate. But this emphasis on active compassion, I learned, could also have its drawbacks. Many years ago I was a social worker. I worked in an environment that was constantly busy and determined to actively find ways to help those in need. This intention was very genuine and had a real sense of care, concern and compassion at its heart. What would sometimes permeate this activity, however, was a kind of compulsion to do things to help even though it was often very unclear what was really needed. From one perspective we could say that our compassion needs to be aligned with the wisdom that knows how best to act and knows the potential consequences. I recall seeing a monk in Bodhgaya, India taking a bag of coins to give to the numerous beggars outside the main Mahabodhi stupa. His act of compassion lead to a near riot as dozens of beggars crowded around him, fighting each other. Within a short space of time some Indian police arrived with long bamboo poles and began to beat the beggars to dispel them.

It is undeniable that compassion needs to engage us with the reality of another's suffering and a real and active willingness to help when we are able and understand what is needed. It is this active dimension of compassion that has stimulated so much worthwhile activity around the world to alleviate sickness, famine, exploitation, political abuse and so on whenever possible. There is a growing movement of what are often known as engaged Buddhists who are very actively trying to do something to help alleviate problems such as climate change. This engagement with the suffering of others and, indeed, with the planet is necessary, worthwhile and laudable. Still, I wish to consider something else here.

When I trained as a psychotherapist, I began to see that how I am able to help another was not always as I thought. The active intention to eliminate the suffering of others needs to be moderated when we are in certain kinds of relationships. I saw that compassion in the context of helping another could also be experienced as a quality of presence that did not actually try to make things better or to find a solution. I learned that my attempts to help and change people's psychological problems was potentially counter to what people really needed. I discovered that healing was facilitated by being truly present with someone with their pain and distress, rather than trying to change it or fix it.

This was a revelation to me and ran contrary to my instinct to do something to relieve people of their pain and suffering. To do so was often to impose my own agenda on another's experience, and that was seldom helpful. I began to see that my desire to relieve the pain of others in this way was more to eliminate or assuage my own distress rather than anything else. It would satisfy my own need to feel I was doing something, but in doing something I was missing the profound nature of compassionate presence as a healing quality in itself. In my therapeutic work I started to recognise a way of being with another while they were in states of distress and pain, a way that did not try to make it different or change it. I learned from my own process of psychotherapy that some of the most powerful healing experiences were simply when someone was present with my pain. What I now recognise is that perhaps the most caring thing we can offer to another person is the quality of compassionate presence.

The therapist's role is not some kind of special activity. It is merely the capacity to be there in a simple, authentic, uncontrived way that does not try to make things be other than as they are. Compassionate presence is in this sense not some exalted state, it is a very natural quality of unconditional presence that feels deeply the pain of another and honours it as it is. I began to learn the extraordinary mystery of what happens when it is possible to genuinely meet someone's pain in this way. This is not something one can fabricate so that we get it right. It is not a creation of some technique; it is more the absence of contrivance, the absence of ideas of what needs to be. Compassionate presence is a disposition which requires us to let go of our need to help, of our agendas and expectations. What feels so difficult is that staying with our own feelings of discomfort and pain is often so hard to bear.

With compassionate presence, a natural flow of healing can unfold. I have described how someone in emotional distress can easily contract into that pain, turning it into horrible suffering. There can be an internal struggle that locks and freezes the natural process of healing. What we may begin to recognise is that when the warmth of compassion is present in the environment, the freezing or contraction can begin to melt, relax and release. There can be a process of letting be or letting go that enables the pain or distress to begin to naturally move through. In guiding meditations, I often use the phrase "allow the feeling, or energy of the feeling, to go where it needs to go". If we can adopt this kind of attitude around suffering, both in ourselves and in the presence of others, the suffering has the space to release. Healing can start to unfold when someone's suffering and pain is truly seen, honoured and blessed. It means that a place of peace can begin to be found, even within pain and fear.

Our capacity for compassionate presence in relation to another's pain, fear and agitation grows with time. It requires that we stay in relationship with and open to the discomfort of another's pain. It means that we do not judge it or feel it should be different. We learn to accept it fully and allow ourselves to be touched by it in a way that does not react and contract from our own place of fear, agitation and the wish to make things OK. Learning to stay totally open in the space of compassion requires we let go of the view that we are there as an agent to *do* something – although of course this does not mean we don't act appropriately when necessary. In that place of openness, compassion is the moisture that enables what needs to unfold towards healing into life, or indeed into dying if that is the journey someone is on.

I have gone to some length describing what I mean by compassionate presence because we begin to discover the pure embodiment of that quality in the practice of Chenrezig. He shows us a way of being that has a steady, unshakeable balance that can hold and bear the suffering of others. Chenrezig, as a manifestation of a bodhisattva's quality of bodhicitta, gives us a particular relationship to the way we can embody compassionate presence in our lives to benefit others. In our meditation practice, we can develop this in two particular ways. One way is to generate the presence of Chenrezig in the heart. The other, known as *self-generation*, is to transform into his nature.

12

Chenrezig in the Heart

OUR RELATIONSHIP to Chenrezig begins in the
context of front-generation outlined in chapter 9,
where we open to his presence in order to receive his
inspiration and blessing. This meditation helps to heal
those aspects of our nature that are in some way
emotionally wounded, particularly through Chenrezig's
compassionate presence. As we begin to discover our own
inner resource of compassion and love, our practice can
evolve. Traditionally this evolution would mean we begin
to explore the process of *self-generation* as I will describe in
the following chapter. To do the self-generation
meditation usually requires some kind of initiation from a
teacher, often in the form of what is called a *jenang*:
permission to practice. For those who do not yet have this
permission, a very practical and beneficial intermediary
meditation is to have Chenrezig seated in the heart. The
power of this practice, when we do it within a deep

meditation and do not merely remain on a conceptual level, should not be underestimated. Some of us may feel that we do not have the capacity to emanate positive qualities like compassion and love. But bringing Chenrezig into the heart can really help this to grow and deepen. When we generate the presence of Chenrezig in our heart chakra, we create a relationship to our innate buddha-nature as an immediate presence. This is a quality that is directly accessed through the heart chakra. As I have said in other contexts, Chenrezig is not an image of our buddha-nature; he is an emanation of it. Bringing his presence alive in the heart activates in us a deep connection to that quality. It is as though we become a vehicle or channel for it to come through us. It is then from that place that we begin to emanate the quality of Chenrezig's compassionate presence.

We begin our meditation from a settled place, resting in the body. Then we gradually open our awareness to its natural spacious clarity, free of concepts. Within that quiet spacious awareness, as we bring Chenrezig into the heart he arises differently to when we use a conceptual recitation practice. It becomes a felt experience within the space of awareness, not a conceptual fabrication.

In meditation, there are two ways we can bring Chenrezig into the heart; one is following the front-generation practice I described earlier. In the other, within the spaciousness of clear awareness we begin to generate Chenrezig directly in the heart. This can be done through becoming aware of a small white syllable HRIH in the heart which radiates light out into the space around. This light invites the blessings of all the buddhas in the form of light, which returns and is absorbed into the HRIH. The HRIH suddenly transforms into the aspect of Chenrezig seated on a lotus and moon disc. He is in the usual form, with one face and four arms, surrounded by an aura of light.

This meditation of Chenrezig arising in the heart is similar to the process I have described in the previous chapter with the practice of tonglen. With him in the heart we begin to open our awareness to those around us to emanate the qualities of compassion and love. Actually, although we may not be aware of it, we emanate all the time. By this I mean that the nature of our inner emotional reality is not confined to just within our skin, it also affects our environment. If we wake up in a foul mood, those we are close to are very likely to pick it up and feel it. If we are in a joyful and happy place, this can be "infectious" and others will feel elevated by our mood. As Lama Yeshe once said, if we are a mess inside then we will emanate a mess outside. If we are in a good, healthy inner space then we will emanate that. Significantly, one of the translations of the Sanskrit word *nirmanakaya* is "emanation body". It is through the vehicle of our physical body that we emanate the quality of the inner energetic process. As I have said, if our inner emotional energy is disturbed or distressed, that will be experienced by others who are sensitive to it. When we hold the presence of Chenrezig in our heart, we can instead begin to emanate his qualities into our environment. When working as a therapist or in any of the caring professions, placing Chenrezig in the heart will definitely enhance our work and the kind of compassionate holding space we are able to offer.

In meditation we have Chenrezig dwelling in our heart, and in his heart is a moon disc upon which stands the syllable HRIH surrounded by the mantra circling counter-clockwise. We can imagine a white light of love and compassion radiating out from his body, filling our physical body. This then begins to emanate from our physical body into the environment around, particularly from our heart. It is helpful to spend some time bringing into our awareness the presence of those we live amongst and work amongst; have a sense of their lives, their struggles and pain as well as their qualities. Letting the heart open in this way, we begin to recite the mantra as a chant or as a whispered recitation, emanating light as we do so.

There is a further meditation we could do at this point, one which is connected to the description I gave of the six realms of existence in chapter 2. It can be very beneficial to consider each of the six realms in turn, reflecting on its particular suffering and the delusion that creates it. We hold the intention to liberate those beings within that realm and then begin to emanate light from Chenrezig in the heart. If you wish, this light can be of the particular colour associated with the syllable of the mantra that purifies the causes of each realm. So we emanate white light from Chenrezig in the heart if we wish to purify the delusion of pride within the deva realm, green to purify the jealousy within the demi-god realm, and so on. As we recite or chant the mantra, we consider that we are liberating the beings in that specific realm from their suffering and causes of suffering.

When I do this practice, or when I guide it in retreats, it can be very helpful to end the practice in the following way. After reciting the mantra for some time, we allow it to become silent. As it does so, we let the mind open to the space of awareness that remains after the sound ceases. We imagine that both Chenrezig and our body's appearance melt into white light, which expands into the space of awareness and emptiness. It is helpful to rest in that experience for as long as possible. This can enable the presence of the quality of Chenrezig as a felt experience to become one with the spacious non-dual nature of the mind. It gives a subtle felt sense of the presence of compassion within spacious awareness that is our mind's nature. Resting in this affirms a deep sense of our innate nature pervaded by the energy of compassion. After some time, our ordinary appearance returns, with the radiant presence of Chenrezig resting in the heart. This process reminds us of the three kayas and that they are there as the constant expression of our buddha-nature coming into form out of emptiness. The spacious nature of our mind's awareness is the basis of *dharmakaya*, the return of our physical appearance is the manifestation of *nirmanakaya*, and the presence of Chenrezig in the heart is the spontaneous expression of *sambhogakaya*. This is conveyed in Figure 1 on page 32.

13

Becoming Chenrezig

ONCE WE ARE FAMILIAR with the processes of meditation where Chenrezig is in the space in front and then at the heart, we can move towards the practice of self-generation. As I began to explain in the previous chapter, this step usually requires that we have some form of initiation to receive permission to meditate in this way. Initiations within the Tibetan tradition can be long and complicated, especially in the context of higher tantra. With a kriya tantra practice of this sort, a relatively simple initiation called a *jenang* (literally: permission to practice) is sufficient to embark fully upon this practice.

Self-generation meditation can begin in a number of ways, some more complex than others. As with the front-generation practice we would usually begin with refuge and bodhicitta prayers and then spend time settling into meditation. The most simple entry into the process of self-generation is to settle in quiet awareness and then become aware of a seed syllable HRIH in the heart. To transform into Chenrezig, we need to first dissolve the appearances of our ordinary reality, as well as our normal self-identity, into emptiness.

We imagine light radiating out from the HRIH, filling the body and then out into the environment around, expanding gradually into the vastness of space. At this point we recall that all ordinary appearances of our world are empty of any enduring substantial nature; they begin to melt into light. This light gradually gathers back until it surrounds the building in which we are seated. This also melts into light and dissolves into the body. As we do this our entanglement with the ordinary appearances of our life have dissolved into emptiness. Then our normal identity and appearance also dissolve as the body melts into light and into the HRIH. Finally, the HRIH dissolves upwards into the *gigu*, the curl on the top, which becomes smaller and smaller until it disappears into emptiness like a clear sky.

Once resting in this spacious emptiness, it is very beneficial to remain there for as long as possible. This can enable a deepening of our capacity to let go of the contracted restlessness in our being that I have described in chapter 5. The reason we experience what I have called this *restlessness of being* is because we are not comfortable with inner space; it causes an existential uncertainty about the nature of our sense of self. Although the self is empty of any inherent enduring nature, our natural habit is to contract and tighten to give us a sense of substance and solidity. The problem is that this contraction does not have anything to hold onto. As a result, our inner response is a

HRIH

subtle existential anxiety. In my own experience of this anxiety, one of the most powerful natural antidotes is the meditation I have just described. At first, it is not uncommon for us to feel some level of fear as our relative world has been dissolved. As we become familiar with this process, however, we will gradually feel more able to let go, relax and open to the spacious nature of awareness and emptiness. We begin to settle and rest in that spaciousness and perhaps begin to heal the roots of our contracted nature.

After we have rested in this spacious emptiness for some time, the intention arises to manifest for the welfare of sentient beings. From within the space of clear awareness beyond form, the bodhicitta intention arises to return to a sense of form in the world. Suddenly, where we are seated there arises an eight-petalled white lotus in the centre of which is a white moon disc. In the centre of the moon disc our consciousness arises as a white syllable HRIH. Our ordinary relative consciousness has returned within the space of non-dual awareness in the aspect of the white HRIH. The HRIH radiates light out into the space around, which invites from dharmakaya the blessings of the buddhas. This light returns, the HRIH transforms and we arise in the aspect of Chenrezig.

While we are in the aspect of Chenrezig, a small syllable HRIH arises in the heart. From that HRIH light radiates out, inviting the compassion and wisdom of all the buddhas into the space in front, also in the form of Chenrezig. This emanation of the buddhas is known as the *jnana*, or "wisdom being", and oneself in the aspect of Chenrezig is known as the *samaya*, or "commitment being". With this wisdom being in the space before us we can make prayers and offerings in a similar way to the front-generation meditation. Or we can simplify this and make a few brief prayers before the wisdom being descends into us. Chenrezig in front comes to the crown of the head and descends, becoming one with our Chenrezig nature. At this point we perform a series of mudras to symbolise the merging of wisdom and symbolic beings. These mudras are connected to four Sanskrit syllables, DZA HUNG BAM HO, each of which has a significance. DZA symbolises that we are hooking or magnetising Chenrezig towards us; HUNG that he comes to the crown of the head; BAM that he descends into us and HO that we become of one nature or one taste. Our Chenrezig nature is now inseparable from that same quality of all the buddhas. With this awareness we hold what is called "divine pride" or confidence in our pristine buddha-nature in the aspect of Chenrezig.

As we rest with the awareness of our Chenrezig quality, we visualise in our crown a white syllable OM, in the throat a red AH and in the heart a white HRIH on a moon disc with the mantra OM MANI PADME HUNG encircling counter-clockwise. From this point we can begin to open our awareness to the presence of sentient beings dwelling on the planet around us. We may choose to keep that focus fairly close to begin with and gradually open to a bigger, wider scope of awareness. To begin it may be good to attune our awareness to the lives of those we are closest to, becoming aware of their struggles and pain but also their qualities. With a sense of love and compassion opening our heart to them, we can begin to emanate light from the heart. This light goes out as a healing, liberating wisdom energy of love and compassion that embraces those around. We hold the aspiration that they may be free of suffering and may be endowed with happiness. Consider those we are close to as well as those we may have difficulties with in our relationships, as it can be this latter group of people that we particularly need to open our hearts to.

We may choose to gradually broaden the scope of our awareness to many different people with us on the planet in their varying degrees and states of suffering. This can include the animals, birds and so on that inhabit the planet with us. In the same way, we emanate a healing light of love and compassion to bring freedom from suffering. Increasingly it feels important to include the planet in this process as we recognise it as a living presence around us; we are totally reliant upon its health and well-being. It is on this level that we may feel a great need at the moment to radiate a healing light to restore the damage that we as a species do to the planet.

A further way of approaching this meditation can be to include what I described in the previous chapter, gradually going through the six realms of existence and purifying their suffering and its cause. This can be especially powerful if we reflect upon the nature of these realms within the human plane of existence. It can be a way of looking at our human condition and recognising the complexity of how we create the causes of suffering in our lives. Having the intention to liberate beings from these various states of suffering can help to strengthen our bodhisattva resolve to remain embodied to serve the welfare of others.

With all of these visualisations it is important that we do not just see this as some kind of nice fantasy that really makes no difference, as if all we are doing is making ourselves feel a bit better. When we do meditation of this sort we need to remember that our practice is functioning on the energetic level of sambhogakaya. We are inhabiting an energetic field that pervades our environment. The three kayas, dharmakaya, sambhogakaya and nirmanakaya, are at the root of our reality and all appearances are an expression of their presence. When we meditate within the dimension of sambhogakaya, our energy effects the environment even though we may not be so aware of it. When we practice Chenrezig, we amplify the effect of our energy because we are attuned to something much greater than our ordinary selves. If we do this in the process of a group retreat, collectively we have an even more potent effect. At this time in our world, we need to be able to do this in order to heal our human species and the planet of the negative shadowy energy that is so destructive. As we awaken our Chenrezig nature we have some power to subtly affect this shadowy energy. We bring a level of wisdom light and compassionate presence into a world that sorely needs it. This is our role as the "baby bodhisattvas" Lama Yeshe once described.

I have said earlier that Chenrezig is the buddha of compassion but that we need to also recognise him as an embodiment of particular qualities of a bodhisattva. As we engage with our practice we are beginning to embody the qualities of a tantric bodhisattva. We become a vehicle or channel for the deepening relationship to our dharmakaya nature to emanate through our sambhogakaya aspect into the embodied form of nirmanakaya. When we place Chenrezig into this flow, we open to an aspect of primordial purity and spontaneous presence[15] that can emanate compassion into the world for the welfare of those struggling in the cycle of existence. As we do this, our growing experience of bodhicitta will express itself through everything we choose to do in our life that serves others. This does not have to be grand and exotic; it can be as simple as the concern and consideration we give to others in our day-to-day relationships. What matters is the quality of compassionate presence and love we begin to emanate.

14

Mahamudra and Chenrezig

WITH ALL OF THE DEITIES I am including in this *Essence of Tantra Series*, the relationship between mahamudra and the deity is very important. I emphasise this because we are looking at deepening our experience of meditation rather than just reciting a sadhana text. This accords with Lama Yeshe's view of what he called the "mahamudra deity" in his book *Becoming the Compassion Buddha*. In *Tasting the Essence of Tantra*, I explain an approach to practice that brings mahamudra into a primary place as the ground from which the deity arises. There is often a tendency to separate these two aspects of practice; the process of arising as the deity is described within what is considered the development or generation stage, and mahamudra is considered an aspect of the completion stage. Because this split is not helpful for the actual experience of meditation in relation to a deity, here we are bringing the two together.

The revered Nyingma master Urgyen Tulku gives a very clear explanation within his book *As it is*, that "The authentic way of practicing development stage is to allow the visualisation to unfold as the natural expression of rigpa." By rigpa he means meditation resting in the nature of mind, as in mahamudra. He says: "Without ever parting from the samadhi of suchness, allow all of the visualisation to take place." He is even more emphatic when he says: "The true development and completion stages are always interconnected. It is not particularly intelligent to try to solely practice development stage without the completion stage, since this leads neither to liberation nor to enlightenment."[16]

A common perspective in the Tibetan tradition is that Chenrezig is not a higher tantra deity, but rather a kriya or lower tantra deity. But this view misrepresents the nature of Chenrezig, who is not a particular class of tantra. It is the *way we practice* that is either lower or higher tantra, not the deity. The practice of Chenrezig can be either within the context of what we might understand as kriya or in a way that is more aligned with an understanding of higher tantra. When we bring together the generation of Chenrezig and the ground of mahamudra meditation, we are unifying the aspects of the development and completion stages clarified by Urgyen Tulku. It is with this emphasis in mind that I am describing a process of meditation within the context of Chenrezig practice where mahamudra is the ground of our experience. When we begin our deity practice from a place of meditation within the spacious nature of awareness, Chenrezig arises as a spontaneous expression of that awareness. As we do this we unify the subtle expression of the deity with the spaciousness of pure awareness. Urgyen Tulku describes this as the "union of pure awareness and spontaneous presence". Spontaneous presence conveys the sense that our arising Chenrezig appearance has no inherent or enduring nature; it is the unfabricated, uncontrived natural expression of our mind's clarity and awareness. This is not determined or fabricated by our ordinary conceptual mind. When we practice in this way we do not leave the quiet openness of our natural awareness; the presence of the deity arises like a cloud within the spaciousness of the sky or a rainbow in space. The cloud is not other than the sky; it appears and can return to the sky. The rainbow is a clear appearance even though it cannot be found. This process of meditation naturally unifies emptiness and appearance.

The practice of a sadhana is an unfolding flow of an imaginal process that evolves to facilitate particular experiences. If we are reading a sadhana this can primarily be just a conceptual experience. When we bring mahamudra into the sadhana, we intentionally slow the process down and quieten the concepts to facilitate a deeper level of meditation. During our sadhana there are also moments when we return to the still clarity of spacious awareness to digest what has unfolded. This gives us the potential to feel the subtle changes and movements of the energy within the body. Rather than trying to get visualisations right and clear, we can increasingly *feel* the quality of Chenrezig in our energy field. As we do this we will find that our meditation of mahamudra deepens along with our deepening experience of Chenrezig. The quality of Chenrezig begins to permeate our nature as a felt effect of our practice.

To bring mahamudra into our practice we need to allow time to start our meditations by settling into the body and then gradually opening to the spacious nature of awareness itself. We begin by resting awareness upon the breath and then gradually shifting to a sense of ground in the body. We then slowly open our awareness to feelings and sensations as they arise and pass within the body. We allow whatever feelings or sensations might arise to be as they are, infusing our awareness with the quality of acceptance, kindness and compassion. We are cultivating the inner felt sense of compassionate presence, free of conceptual thinking.

As this meditation becomes more established we will feel a softening and quietening of how we rest within ourselves. This creates an environment of care and kindness around our feelings, especially when we are distressed or in pain, allowing them the space to be there with greater acceptance. We can soften the habit of either contracting into our feelings or pushing them away. With greater kindness and compassion, we begin to relax in ourselves and are able to be more spacious and less contracted. There is then less tension and a greater sense of inner peace and contentment, which can filter out into our life and relationships. We are beginning to transform the *restlessness of being* into a sense of ease and spaciousness. This then enables us to soften and relax the contraction around our sense of self, which in turn enables us also to begin to open to others more fully.

As we gradually rest in this more spacious, compassionate inner environment, we are creating the conditions for opening into the practice of mahamudra. As our body rests and settles, we slowly open to the natural spacious clarity of awareness itself. Awareness that is empty of any enduring nature. Meditation in this way can be the perfect antidote to our *restlessness of being* because we are resting in spacious awareness permeated with compassion. Once established, it is into that space of awareness that we can bring Chenrezig, recognising that his presence is not other than the nature of our mind. This is the "union of pure awareness and spontaneous presence" described by Urgyen Tulku. Because Chenrezig is an emanation of the compassion of all the buddhas, when we bring him into the space of our awareness we invite a quality that is possibly the most powerful expression of compassionate presence we may ever feel. This is not just a fantasy or something we are making up. Chenrezig is a vibrant emanation of buddha-nature.

In meditation when we are practicing Chenrezig, it is extremely important – just as it is in mahamudra – to slow the process down and give ourselves time to rest in the felt sense of his presence. In my own experience of reciting traditional sadhanas relating to Chenrezig, often very little time is spent really resting in the felt sense of the relationship. This can mean we do not give ourselves time to open to receive Chenrezig's blessing deeply into our body and feeling. If we can meditate in a way that is less the recitation of a sadhana text and more a deeper level of meditation, then we can begin to feel the impact of his presence. As Lama Yeshe and Urgyen Tulku both emphasised, if we can rest in the nature of clear awareness that comes from mahamudra and open to the presence of Chenrezig we will be deeply touched by his presence.

In our sadhana meditation, one place where this deeper connection to the felt sense of Chenrezig within the spacious nature of mahamudra can really become apparent is following the recitation or chant of the mantra. When the sound of the mantra stops, whether in the context of front-generation or self-generation, we need to rest in the silence that remains and open to the spacious nature of awareness itself. This spaciousness will be pervaded by the subtle felt sense of the quality of Chenrezig within our energy-body. The space that follows the mantra is sometimes called "samadhi at the end of sound", and this is a time when we can directly experience the pristine nature of our mind. The mantra has the effect of clearing the mind of disturbance such that, for a while, we can simply drop into the space of mahamudra.

The combination of Chenrezig and mahamudra offers us the possibility of resting in a space of compassionate presence that begins to heal our restlessness of being. We can also begin to soften and let go of the contracted wounding we experience around our sense of self. As we feel more at ease in our sense of being, we will also be able to respond to others from a deeper place of love and openness. From this place our quality of bodhicitta will naturally grow.

In each of the meditations that follow, mahamudra is the basis from which the various practices unfold. I will be describing the evolution of a process that is best experienced within that space of meditation. To do this I would recommend gradually memorising the descriptions so that you do not need to read them. Then, as you become more familiar with the evolution of the practices, begin to drop some of the words to make it a more integrated experience. In this way you can also make subtle changes to how the meditations unfold. The prayers I have used can also be adapted to suit your own inclination. Begin to shape the practices to make them your experience.

Meditation 1: Front-Generation

Following a period of meditation to bring awareness into the body and settle, begin to open to the natural spaciousness of awareness. Then recite the refuge prayer:

SANG.GYE CHO.DANG TSOG.KYI CHOG
NAM LA
J'ANG.CHUB BAR.DU DAG.NYI KYAB SU CHI
DAG.GI JIN.TSOG GYI.PE SO.NAM KYI
DRO.LA PEN.CHIR SANG.GYE DRUB.PAR
SHOG

"I go for refuge until I am enlightened, to the Buddha, Dharma and the supreme community. Through the virtues of giving and other perfections, may I swiftly attain enlightenment for the benefit of all sentient beings."

Return to the spaciousness of awareness and rest in meditation for a while to drop beneath the conceptual mind.

Within that space of awareness, in the space before you at the level of the forehead there arises an eight-petalled white lotus, in the centre of which is a circular white moon disc lying flat. Standing in the centre of the moon disc is a white flame marked by a seed syllable HRIH. This symbolises your own innate primordially pure buddha-nature, your buddha potential.

HRIH

Light radiates from the flame and HRIH out into the universe, inviting from dharmakaya the essence of all the buddhas' enlightened compassion and wisdom in the aspect of countless tiny white Chenrezigs that absorb back into the flame and HRIH like snowflakes melting.

The flame and HRIH become endowed with powerful, vibrant light energy and suddenly transform into the aspect of Chenrezig, the buddha of compassion. He is white in colour, seated in the full lotus posture with one face and four arms. His first two hands are held at the heart with palms together, holding a piece of blue lapis lazuli. His second right hand holds at the right side of his head a crystal rosary. His second left hand, at the left side of his head, holds the stem of a lotus flower. Dressed in robes of silk and adorned with ornaments of gold and precious jewels, his hair is tied in a topknot and loose across his shoulders. Smiling with narrow compassionate eyes like a loving parent for his only child, he is surrounded by an aura of light.

"Precious Chenrezig who is the essence of my own innate buddha potential inseparable from that of all the buddhas; who is the embodiment of compassion and the source of blessing and inspiration, of healing and transformation; as my guide and protector, to you I go for refuge."

Then make offerings to Chenrezig:
OM ARYA CHENREZIG SAPARIWARA ARGHAM PRATITSA HUM SVAHA (water for drinking)
OM ARYA CHENREZIG SAPARIWARA PADYAM PRATITSA HUM SVAHA (water for washing)
OM ARYA CHENREZIG SAPARIWARA PUSHPE PRATITSA HUM SVAHA (flowers)
OM ARYA CHENREZIG SAPARIWARA DUPE PRATITSA HUM SVAHA (incense)
OM ARYA CHENREZIG SAPARIWARA ALOKE PRATITSA HUM SVAHA (lights)
OM ARYA CHENREZIG SAPARIWARA GHANDE PRATITSA HUM SVAHA (perfume)
OM ARYA CHENREZIG SAPARIWARA NAIVIDYA PRATITSA HUM SVAHA (food)
OM ARYA CHENREZIG SAPARIWARA SHABDA PRATITSA HUM SVAHA (music)

Make these offerings with a heart-felt sense of gratitude for the presence of Chenrezig as well as to support any requests you may make for particular results of practice. Then make requests for Chenrezig's blessings:

"Noble Chenrezig, I request you to bestow your blessings to purify and heal all my negativity, sickness, harmful interferences, life hindrances and emotional afflictions and to bestow the qualities of compassion, loving kindness, openness and acceptance that I may awaken for the benefit of all sentient beings."

You can add to this your own prayers that may relate to particular things you may need to clear or wish to develop.

Before you perform the mantra recitation, spend some time tuning in to the relationship with Chenrezig. It is helpful to allow time to receive light energy of compassion emanating from his heart into you so that you feel a deepening sense of closeness and his presence.

(At this point you can follow a relatively simple form of practice describe here, or you can follow the heart-healing meditation I have suggested in chapter 9).

Mantra Recitation:

OM

In Chenrezig's crown is a white syllable OM, in his throat a red AH and in his heart a white HRIH on a moon disc with the mantra encircling. As you recite the mantra, light radiates out from the syllables of the mantra, the HRIH and every atom of Chenrezig's body. This light of loving kindness and compassion washes down through you, cleansing and healing negativity and awakening the qualities you wish for.

OM MANI PADME HUM (recite at least 108 times)

AH

Following the mantra recitation, let go into the natural clarity of awareness and the quality of feeling that is left.

After a while, restore your awareness of the radiant presence of Chenrezig in the space before you. He then comes to the crown of your head and, becoming smaller and smaller, descends through your crown to become seated in your heart chakra as your own inner Chenrezig nature. From your heart a light of compassion and acceptance radiates out, filling your entire body. Rest with this awareness for a few minutes.

Dedication:

"May whatever virtuous energy I generate through this practice enable me to awaken to my full buddha potential in order to be of lasting benefit to every living being without exception, to enable them to also awaken to their full potential."

*****

Meditation 2: Heart-Generation

(This meditation can follow on from the front-generation practice or be done independently. If you do it independently, begin as follows.)

Begin by settling on the breath and resting into the body. As your mind quietens, let your awareness open. After a while, become aware of a small white eight-petalled lotus in your heart with a moon disc resting at its centre. In the centre of the moon disc stands a white flame marked by a syllable HRIH. Light radiates out from the flame and HRIH into the space around and invites from dharmakaya the blessing of the buddhas, which returns in the form of light. The flame blazes with light and suddenly transforms into the aspect of Chenrezig in your heart. His appearance is as in the previous meditation. In his crown is a white OM, in his throat a red AH, and in his heart a white HRIH on a moon disc with the mantra encircling.

Spend some time with this awareness of Chenrezig in your heart. Then begin to open your awareness to those living around you. Those you are close to, those you work amongst and who inhabit the planet with us. Also to the planet itself. Begin to quietly whisper the mantra, allowing the vibrancy of Chenrezig to grow as though you are gathering or generating his energy within your heart. After some time, let that light energy fill your body and then begin to radiate out into the world around. Have the feeling that this light of love and compassion goes to those around you, healing, transforming and awakening them and freeing them from suffering.

After some time, let the mantra stop and imagine that Chenrezig and your body dissolve into vibrant light which expands into the vastness of space, into the space of awareness and emptiness. Rest in that space of non-duality for as long as you can. Eventually your ordinary appearance returns, and at your heart is the radiant presence of Chenrezig. Finish with your dedication prayers.

*****

Meditation 3: Self-Generation

(The self-generation practice is for those who have received the necessary *jenang*, or permission to practice.* With this meditation in particular, it is helpful to bring together the deity process with the meditation of mahamudra. This will enable a deeper level of felt experience with less emphasis on the conceptual process.)

Spend a period of time settling and then recite the refuge prayer:

SANG.GYE CHO.DANG TSOG.KYI CHOG
NAM LA
J'ANG.CHUB BAR.DU DAG.NYI KYAB SU CHI
DAG.GI JIN.TSOG GYI.PE SO.NAM KYI
DRO.LA PEN.CHIR SANG.GYE DRUB.PAR
SHOG

"I go for refuge until I am enlightened, to the Buddha, Dharma and the supreme community. Through the virtues of giving and other perfections, may I swiftly attain enlightenment for the benefit of all sentient beings."

Follow this with a period of meditation to bring awareness into the body to settle, then begin to open to the natural spaciousness of awareness. Spend a good period of time in this settling process so that what follows can naturally emerge within the space of meditation.

In your heart there arises a small drop of light about the size of a pea. Vibrant light begins to radiate out from this drop, filling your body. This light radiates out from your body and fills the room, and whatever it touches becomes in the nature of light while retaining its appearance. The light expands, encompassing the building, the environment around, and gradually out to embrace the entire planet and out into the universe.

All universal phenomena, lacking inherent substantiality, being by nature empty, begin to melt into light, which absorbs into the planet. The planet also melts into light and dissolves into the surrounding environment, which dissolves into this building, into the room. Then the room melts into light and dissolves into your body, which also melts into light and dissolves into the drop in the heart. The drop becomes smaller and smaller until all relative appearances dissolve into emptiness like a clear sky, into dharmakaya. Rest in this space of empty awareness for some time.

Within the clarity of non-dual awareness, the intention arises to manifest for the benefit of sentient beings.

Suddenly within the sphere of emptiness, where you are seated there arises an eight-petalled white lotus, in the centre of which is a circular white moon disc lying flat. In the centre of the moon disc your consciousness suddenly arises as a white seed syllable HRIH which blazes with light, and instantly you arise as Chenrezig, the buddha of compassion. Your body is white in colour, seated in the full lotus posture with one face and four arms. Your first two hands are held at the heart with palms together, holding a blue lapis lazuli. Your second right hand holds a crystal rosary at the right side of your head. Your second left hand holds the stem of a lotus flower blooming at the left side of your head. Dressed in robes of silk and adorned with ornaments of gold and precious jewels, your hair is tied in a topknot and loose across the shoulders. Smiling with narrow, compassionate eyes you are surrounded by an aura of light.

In your crown is a white syllable OM, in your throat a red AH, and in your heart a white HRIH. From the HRIH in your heart light radiates out, invoking from dharmakaya the essence of the buddhas' enlightened compassion and wisdom in the form of the "wisdom being" Chenrezig who instantly arises in the space before you appearing identical to yourself.

"Precious Chenrezig, who is the essence of all the buddhas' awakened compassion and wisdom, the source of healing and transformation, of blessing and inspiration; as my guide and protector, to you I go for refuge."

The wisdom being Chenrezig comes to the crown of your head and descends into you.
DZA HUM BAM HO

Your Chenrezig nature is inseparable from the essence of all the buddhas.

Mantra Recitation:

In your heart, the syllable HRIH stands on a moon disc with the mantra encircling counter-clockwise.

As you recite the mantra, light radiates out from the syllables of the mantra, the HRIH and every atom of your Chenrezig body. This light of loving kindness and compassion goes out to the countless sentient beings around you, eliminating the sufferings of sentient beings in the world and bringing everlasting peaceful happiness.

OM MANI PADME HUM (recite at least 108 times)

Following the mantra recitation, let go into the natural clarity of awareness and the quality of feeling that is left while retaining an awareness of your radiant Chenrezig appearance with divine confidence.

Dedication:

May whatever virtuous energy I generate through this practice enable me to awaken to my full buddha potential in order to be of lasting benefit to every living being without exception, to enable them to also awaken to their full potential.

(This self-generation practice has been created by Rob Preece from an original source. It is only available to those who have received permission to practice this tantra of Chenrezig and must not be reproduced without permission. 13th March 2005)

Notes

[1] H.H. Dalai Lama, *Beyond Religion: Ethics for a Whole World.*

[2] Rob Preece, *Heart Essence;* chapter 4, "Equanimity".

[3] Shantideva, *Guide to the Bodhisattva's Way of Life (Bodhisattvacaryavatara)*, chapter 1, verse 10.

[4] Togme Zangpo, *The 37 Practices of All Buddhas' Sons*, verse 10

[5] *Kaya* is Sanskrit for "body", as in a body of water.

[6] Shantideva, *Guide (Bodhisattvacaryavatara)*, chapter 10, Dedication, verse 55.

[7] C.G. Jung, *The Archetypes and the Collective Unconscious*, p. 92.

[8] The term "good enough mother" is one D.W. Winnicott used frequently in his writing e.g. in *Home Is Where We Start From: Essays by a Psychoanalyst.*

[9] I refer to the work of Lake, Sills and others who challenged Freud's view that there was no self-reference until after birth. See F. Lake, *Studies in Constricted Confusion: Exploration of a Pre- and Perinatal Paradigm.*

[10] Michael Washburn, *The Ego and the Dynamic Ground,* chapter 2.

[11] Peter Levine, *Waking the Tiger* and *In an Unspoken Voice.*

[12] Stephen Batchelor, *Flight: An Existential Conception of Buddhism.*

[13] See Peter Levine, *Waking the Tiger* and *In an Unspoken voice.*

[14] See Rob Preece, *Heart Essence: Enhancing Qualities of the Awakening Mind.*

[15] "Without leaving the empty suchness samadhi of rigpa behind, the compassionate illumination of spontaneous presence unfolds unobstructedly from the primordially pure essence." From Urgyen Tulku's *As It Is,* p.191.

[16] Urgyen Tulku, *As It Is,* p.110.

Arhant	Skt. One who has become liberated from the cycle of existence.
Asura	Skt. A demi-god or titan. One of the six realms of existence.
Avalokiteshvara	Skt. (Tib. Chenrezig.) One of the Buddha's foremost disciples. Also known as the buddha of compassion.
Bodhicitta	Skt. The awakening mind or heart essence; the intention to awaken for the welfare of sentient beings.
Bodhisattva	Skt. One who is engaged in the path to awaken for the welfare of sentient beings. The awakening warrior.
Bodhisattva-caryavatara	Skt. A text composed by the Indian saint Shanitideva called, in English, "Guide to the Bodhisattva's Way of Life".
Brahmavihara	Skt. Literally: the abode of Brahma; a series known as the four immeasurables.
Chakra	Skt. Literally: wheel; conjunction of channels in the central channel of the energy-body.
Chenrezig	Tib. (Skt. Avalokiteshvara.) The buddha of compassion.

Dakdsin	Tib. Ego-grasping; the root of suffering.
Deva	Skt. A god. One of the six realms of existence.
Dharma	Skt. Literally: truth or true; the Buddha's teachings.
Dharmakaya	Skt. The "wisdom body" or "truth-body" of a buddha.
Dochak	Tib. Grasping.
Dzogchen	Tib. Literally: great completion; meditation on the natural clarity of the mind.
Guanyin	Chinese. Also known as Kannon in Japan. A female form of Avalokiteshvara.
Guru	Tib. Lama; teacher.
Heart Sutra	A teaching of the Buddha through the channel of Avalokiteshvara.
Individuation	Jungian term: the process of self-actualisation (not individualism).
Jenang	Tib. Permission to practice. A basic level of initiation into deity practice.
Jinlab	Tib. Literally: waves of inspiring energy. Often translated as "blessing".
Kaya	Skt. Literally: body, as in a body of water.

Khakkhara	Skt. Sounding stick. A staff carried by monks at the time of the Buddha to notify other creatures of their presence.
Kriya tantra	Skt. Action tantra. The basic level of the four levels of tantra.
Mahakaruna	Skt. Great compassion.
Mahamudra	Skt. Meditation on the mind's innate clarity.
Manjushri	Skt. One of the Buddha's principle disciples known as the buddha of wisdom.
Mala	Skt. (Tib. Trengwa) A rosary for counting mantras, usually with 108 beads.
Mudra	Skt. A symbolic gesture or expression of the body, particularly of the hands.
Namtok	Tib. Discursive chatter of the mind.
Narak	Skt. Hell realm. One of the six realms of existence.
Nirmanakaya	Skt. The "emanation body" or "manifestation body" of a buddha.
Preta	Skt. Wandering spirit. One of the six realms of existence.
Rigpa	Tib. Literally to see. A term used for pure awareness, the nature of the mind, within the dzogchen tradition.
Sadhana	Skt. Method of accomplishment of a tantric deity.

Samadhi	Skt. Tranquil abiding.
Samaya	Skt. Commitment.
Sambhogakaya	Skt. The "enjoyment body", or "purified energy-body" of a buddha.
Samsara	Skt. The cycle of existence.
Self	Jungian term: the centre of our totality. Archetypal root of meaning.
Shantideva	Skt. A highly revered 11th-century Indian scholar.
Soklung	Tib. Disturbance of the energy-winds associated with the heart chakra.
Suchness	A term equivalent to emptiness.
Tantra	Skt. The Buddha's esoteric teaching.
Tara	Skt. A female tantric meditation deity, the embodiment of active compassion and all-accomplishing wisdom.
Thangka	Tib. A Tibetan icon painting.
Tonglen	Tib. Literally: Giving and taking. A meditation practice for the cultivation of compassion and love.
Tulku	Tib. (Skt. Nirmanakaya.) A reincarnated lama, usually called Rinpoche.
Vajrapani	Skt. One of the Buddha's disciples who had the role of a protector, later becoming the embodiment of the power of the awakened mind.

Bibliography

Arya Maitreya and Asanga. *The Changeless Nature: The Mahayana Uttara Tantra Shastra.* Trans. Ken and Katia Holmes. Eskdalemuir: Kagyu Samye Ling, 1985.

Batchelor, Stephen. *Flight: An Existential Conception of Buddhism.* Delhi Buddhist Publication Society, 1984.

Dalai Lama. *Beyond Religion, Ethics for a Whole World.* London: Rider, 2012.

Dalai Lama. *Essence of the Heart Sutra.* Trans. and ed. Thupten Jinpa. Boston: Wisdom Publications, 2005.

Dalai Lama. *Stages of Meditation.* Ithaca: Snow Lion Publications, 2001.

Dalai Lama & Alexander Berzin. *The Gelug/Kagyu Tradition of Mahamudra.* Ithaca: Snow Lion Publications, 1997.

Dhargyey, Geshe Ngawang. *The Tibetan Tradition of Mental Development.* Dharamsala: Library of Tibetan Works and Archives, 1974.

Dzogchen Ponlop. *Wild Awakening: The Heart of Mahamudra and Dzogchen.* Boston: Shambhala Publications, 2003.

Epstein, Dr Mark. *Going to Pieces Without Falling Apart: A Buddhist Perspective on Wholeness.* London: Thorsons, 1998.

Jacobi, Jolande. *Complex/Archetype/Symbol in the Psychology of C. G. Jung.* Trans. Ralph Manheim. Princeton:

Princeton University Press/Bollingen Foundation, 1971.

Jung, C.G. *Alchemical Studies*. Ed. and trans. Gerhard Adler and R. F. C. Hull. The Collected Works of C. G. Jung. Vol. 13. Princeton: Princeton University Press/Bollingen Foundation, 1983.

Jung, C.G. *The Archetypes and the Collective Unconscious*. Ed. and trans. Gerhard Adler and R. F. C. Hull. The Collected Works of C. G. Jung. Vol. 9, Part 1. Princeton: Princeton University Press/Bollingen Foundation, 1981.

Jung, C.G., ed. *Man and His Symbols*. New York: Anchor Books, Doubleday, 1964.

Jung, C.G. *Psychology and Alchemy*. Ed. and trans. Gerhard Adler and R. F. C. Hull. The Collected Works of C. G. Jung. Vol. 12. Princeton: Princeton University Press/Bollingen Foundation, 1980.

Jung, C.G. *Psychology and Religion: West and East*. Ed. and trans. Gerhard Adler and R. F. C. Hull. The Collected Works of C. G. Jung. Vol. 11. Princeton: Princeton University Press/Bollingen Foundation, 1970.

Lake, F. *Studies in Constricted Confusion: Exploration of a Pre and Perinatal Paradigm*. Oxford: The Clinical Theology Association, 1979.

Levine, Peter A. *In an Unspoken Voice: How the Body Releases Trauma and Restores Goodness*. Berkeley: North Atlantic Books, 2010.

Levine, Peter A. *Waking the Tiger*. Berkeley: North Atlantic Books, 1997.

Long Chen Pa. *Kindly Bent to Ease Us. Part One: Mind*. Trans. and annot. Herbert V Guenther. Emeryville: Dharma Publishing, 1975.

Long Chen Rab Jampa, H.H. Dudjom Rinpoche, Beru Khyentze Rinpoche. *The Four Themed Precious Garland*.

Dharamsala: Library of Tibetan Works and Archives, 1979.

Preece, Rob. *The Courage to Feel*. Ithaca: Snow Lion Publications, 2009.

Preece, Rob. *Heart Essence: Enhancing Qualities of the Awakening Mind*. Devon: Mudra Publications, 2022.

Preece, Rob. *Preparing for Tantra: Creating the Psychological Ground for Practice*. Ithaca: Snow Lion Publications, 2011.

Preece, Rob. *The Psychology of Buddhist Tantra*. Ithaca: Snow Lion Publications, 2006.

Preece, Rob. *Tasting the Essence of Tantra: Buddhist Meditation for Contemporary Western Life*. Devon: Mudra Publications, 2018.

Preece, Rob. *The Wisdom of Imperfection*. Ithaca: Snow Lion Publications, 2006.

Rabten, Geshe. *The Essential Nectar: Meditations on the Buddhist Path*. Boston: Wisdom Publications, 1984.

Rabten, Geshe. *The Preliminary Practices of Tibetan Buddhism*. Dharamsala: Library of Tibetan Works and Archives, 1974.

Shantideva: *Guide to the Bodhisattva's Way of Life*. Trans. Stephen Bachelor. Dharamsala: Library of Tibetan Works and Archives,1979.

Sills, Franklin. *Being and Becoming: Psychodynamics, Buddhism, and the Origins of Selfhood*. Berkeley: North Atlantic Books, 2009.

Sonam Rinchen, Geshe. *The Three Principle Aspects of the Path*. Ithaca: Snow Lion Publications, 1999.

Tarthang Tulku. *Gesture of Balance*. Berkeley: Dharma Publishing, 1977.

Tarthang Tulku. *The Joy of Being*. California: Dharma Publishing, 2006.

Thrangu, Khenchen Rinpoche. *Essentials of Mahamudra*.

Boston: Wisdom Publications, 2004.

Thrangu, Khenchen Rinpoche. *An Ocean of the Ultimate Meaning: Teachings on Mahamudra.* Boston: Shambhala Publications, 2004.

Togme Zangpo. *The Thirty-Seven Practices of All Buddhas Sons.* Dharamsala: Translation Bureau of the Library of Tibetan Works and Archives, 1975.

Tsongkhapa. *Three Principal Aspects of the Path.* Trans. Alexander Berzin. Dharamsala: Library of Tibetan Works and Archives, 1982.

Tulku Urgyen Rinpoche. *As It Is,* Hong Kong: Rangjung Yeshe Publications, 1999.

Van der Kolk, Bessel. *The Body Keeps the Score: Mind, Brain and Body in the Transformation of Trauma.* UK: Penguin Books, 2014.

Washburn, Michael. *The Ego and the Dynamic Ground: A Transpersonal Theory of Human Development.* Albany: State University of New York Press, 1995.

Welwood, John. *Awakening the Heart: East/West Approaches to Psychotherapy and the Healing Relationship.* Boston: Shambala, 1985.

Welwood, John. *Towards a Psychology of Awakening: Buddhism, Psychotherapy, and the Path of Personal and Spiritual Transformation.* Boston: Shambala, 2002.

Winnicott, D.W. *Home Is Where We Start From: Essays by a Psychoanalyst.* Harmondsworth: Penguin Books Ltd, 1986.

Winnicott, D.W. *The Maturational Processes and the Facilitating Environment: Studies in the Theory of Emotional Development.* London: Karnac Books Ltd, 1965.

Yeshe, Lama Thubten. *Becoming the Compassion Buddha.* Boston: Wisdom Publications, 2003.

Yeshe, Lama Thubten. *Mahamudra.* Boston: Wisdom Publications, 1981.

About the Author

Following an apprenticeship in electronics engineering Rob Preece went to university to study psychology. It was at this time he met both the work of C.G. Jung and Buddhism. After university, a period of travel led him to Nepal where, in 1973, he met his teachers Lama Thubten Yeshe and Lama Zopa Rinpoche.

Rob was a social worker for 3 years and then, in 1976, he was part of a small group that founded a Buddhist centre in the UK for his Tibetan teachers. For the next four years he studied the foundations of Tibetan practice in that Buddhist community. In 1980 he returned to India and was in retreat for much of the next five years. This gave him a chance to explore the practices of the tantric tradition in some depth, meditating under the guidance of Lama Yeshe, Zopa Rinpoche and Gen Jhampa Wangdu in particular. While in India he was fortunate enough to receive teachings and tantric empowerments from lamas such as H.H. Dalai Lama, Song Rinpoche, Lati Rinpoche and many others. It also gave him the opportunity to learn thangka (tantric icon) painting. Rob has also received dzogchen teachings from H.H. Dudjom Rinpoche, then head of the Nyingma tradition, and more recently from Tsok Nyi Rinpoche.

After returning to the West Rob trained as a psychotherapist with the Centre for Transpersonal Psychology in London. This began the process of bringing together the two worlds of Buddhism and Jungian psychology as a practicing psychotherapist. Since 1985 he has been leading meditation retreats following the guidance of his teachers. Lama Yeshe was particularly influential in this, supporting his integration of a more Western approach. Rob's one-to-one work is now principally spiritual mentoring, bringing together his experience of both Eastern and Western approaches.

Rob leads meditation retreats in the UK, Europe and the US. In the UK, some of these retreats incorporate a movement practice facilitated by his wife Anna. As a father of two sons, an experienced thangka painter and a keen gardener he tries to ground Buddhist practice in a creative practical lifestyle. He is the author of many books bridging the Tibetan tradition with Western psychology, intended to support Buddhist practice in contemporary life. These include: *The Psychology of Buddhist Tantra*; *The Wisdom of Imperfection*; *The Courage to Feel*; *Preparing for Tantra*; *Feeling Wisdom* and *Tasting the Essence of Tantra*.

Essence of Tantra Series

In this new series of books following his **Tasting the Essence of Tantra,** Rob takes specific areas of tantra into more depth. He continues to follow the principles first taught by his teacher Lama Thubten Yeshe, bringing together the worlds of Western psychology and Buddhist understanding. It is his unique depth of experience of both worlds that gives this series its aliveness and creativity. New and experienced practitioners alike will find these books invaluable in deepening the effectiveness of the tantric path.

The series will contain the following books:

The Mandala and Visions of Wholeness: Within Tibetan Buddhism and Jungian Psychology

Heart Essence: Enhancing Qualities of the Awakening Mind

Manjushri: The Creative Expression of Wisdom

Chenrezig: Embodying Compassionate Presence

Vajrapani: Clarifying our Relationship to Power

Green Tara: Embodying Dynamic Compassion

For information relating to these books and Rob's work, go to
www.mudra.co.uk
If you have enjoyed this book, please feel free to put a review on Amazon.